52
more
OFFBEAT TEXAS
STOPS

Published in 1997 by
Phillips Productions, Inc.
1323 N. Stemmons
Dallas, TX 75207

Printed in Hong Kong by Regent Publishing Services Limited

First Edition

Library of Congress Cataloging in Publication Data
52 More Offbeat Texas Stops
Traveling with Bob Phillips, Texas Country Reporter
97-091943
ISBN 0-9636541-5-2

Designed by Jerry Price

52 more

OFFBEAT TEXAS STOPS

TRAVELING WITH
BOB PHILLIPS
TEXAS COUNTRY REPORTER

By Bob Phillips

1323 N. Stemmons
Dallas, TX 75207

Contents

These are approximate locations of the 52 stops.

Dedication

For my producer and friend Jason Anderson,
who for 17 years has been reminding me
of what it is we're trying to do
and how best to go about doing it.

Acknowledgments

Once again, this is a book that would never have been written were it not for M'Layne Murphy. She was the one who said we had to do it and she was the one who made sure we did. Without her we would have spent a lot of time talking about it, and as our colleague Brian Hawkins says, "Talkin' about it don't get it done."

I have spent the better part of my life traveling Texas' backroads, but I never take notes because I prefer to write from the heart and feel the facts often get in the way of good emotion. Thank goodness, then, that I had M'Layne not only to push this book through but to check my facts and make lots of corrections where my memory failed me.

Though this is her first experience at doing so, one could not ask for a better editor than Brooke Maples, who doubles as a producer on our television show and also serves as a friend and close advisor. The design of this book is the work of our good friend Jerry Price. Most of the pictures inside the book are video images taken from our *Texas Country Reporter* television show and were computer enhanced by artist Gina Six.

I also owe thanks to Martin Perry, Jason Anderson and Christy Carnes who covered for me while I sat for hours at the computer, and to all the other folks who have traveled with me on the road for 25 years. And a heartfelt thanks to the people who opened up their homes and their hearts and allowed us to tell their stories to you.

Special thanks to the following:

Festival Hill, Round Top: photo, page 19
Boerne Village Band, Boerne: photo, page 44
Larry Piltz, Austin: photo, page 47
Institute of Texan Cultures, San Antonio: photo, page 52
Art Car Parade, Houston: photo, page 72
Edison Museum, Beaumont: photo, page 78
Sulphur Springs CVB: photo, page 86
Paris CVB/Linda Suarez: photo, page 88
Big Bill Johnson, "I'm a Drywall Man:" lyrics, page 91
Thistle Hill, Fort Worth: photo, page 97
Castro County News, Dimmitt/Scott Brockman: photo 125
Carl Walz, Inc., St. Louis, Missouri: photo frame, cover
Trey Hill, Express Typesetting Co., Inc.: typesetting

The famous Texas Country Reporter Bridge (aka Regency Bridge)

Preface

Funny how a *job* can sometimes turn into a *career*. This one did just that sometime in the past quarter-century while I wasn't looking. I started working in television at 18 years old while in my first year of college. Some of the old-timers around the newsroom at that Dallas television station called me *the kid*. Today, some of the folks who work with me at my production company call me *the old-timer*. Whatever the title, I've been involved in collecting stories on the backroads of Texas for more than 25 years now. I sent my tales back and the television stations just kept putting them on the air. Lucky for me. I never had to get a real job.

It didn't take long for me to realize that Texas has a special place in the hearts of a lot of people. It is a magical, mythical place and folks want to see it. If they don't know which direction to go, sometimes they ask me. One thing you get good at after driving the same state for this long is giving directions. A few years ago we published our first travel book, *52 Offbeat Texas Stops*. It was an instant bestseller, and therefore, an instant success. We called them "stops" because most of the destinations were intended to be just that - a place to stop and explore for a short while. After they had stopped at all our stops, folks wanted more. *52 MORE Offbeat Texas Stops* is our attempt at a follow-up, but we've also tried to expand things this time out. Along with the *Stops* we've listed our *Best Bets*, other things we think you'll find interesting while you're in the area. So this book is more than a list of 52 places - It is a true Texas guidebook to the unknown, unusual and unexplored all over the state.

The best way to use this book is to pick out the area you want to visit, decide when you want to go there, then plan your trip using the information we offer here. By no means have we attempted to tell you every place there is to visit, everything there is to do at each destination. You can usually get that list from the local chamber of commerce. Our goal is to tell you about the places we discovered on our television program or the places we found to be extra special in some way so you can truly experience the offbeat Texas. After you get there, look around. You'll be amazed at what you will discover on your own. If there has been a secret to finding our stories all these years, it is just that - Keep your eyes open and watch for those things that are different and interesting. The chapters in the book are arranged in a somewhat reasonable order, starting in Central Texas and working our way around the state in a convoluted counter-clockwise pattern. In most cases you will find the stops just before and just after your destination are close by, so you may want to combine several stops into one trip.

Be sure you pay attention to the days and hours of operation and the "call first" requests. Some of the folks aren't really set up to receive lots of visitors, but they have agreed to do so because we asked. We've found there is a common politeness about the Texans we run across and ask you to return the favor to them.

One more thing - everyone wants to know about *The Bridge*. "The Bridge" refers to the shot of an old suspension bridge we show during the open to our television program each week. We ran across it several years ago and ever since, people have been asking how to get there. It's on a dirt road in what used to be Regency, Texas, thus the name Regency Bridge. It crosses the Colorado River. From Goldthwaite, Texas, take Highway 574 west for about 15 miles until Highway 573 intersects the road on your right. Continue on 574 and a short distance later you will see a dirt road on your left. Turn there and you'll see *The Bridge* a few miles south of 574. You'll find it easier to locate if you'll make use of the *The Roads of Texas* atlas. Regency Bridge is on page 104.

Thanks for going with us on the backroads once again. We always appreciate your company. Happy Traveling!

Bob Phillips

Something Hot for the Road

We'll begin our tour of Texas in the area where Texas began. Actually, you might say there were two such beginnings for Texas in this area. Part of the original Stephen F. Austin land grant, which brought colonists to Texas, is here in Grimes County. In fact, Andrew Robinson, first of Austin's colonists, set up a ferry nearby in 1822. For those who don't know, Austin was an early Texan who came to be known as the "Father of Texas." The other beginning of which we speak is the one which occurred in what would come to be known as Washington County, just a few miles from Navasota, where in 1836, Texas declared her independence from Mexico and drafted the constitution for the new republic. Had those events not happened, we would not be writing this book.

Stop #1
Navasota, Texas

You might expect then that Stop Number One would be a visit to a local Texas history museum or some Texas revolutionary battlefield and yes, those will be included, too. But to get started on this journey, we suggest you make your way to Navasota, Texas, where you can find and sample some of Buck's Hot Carrots.

If she's told him once, she's told him a thousand times: Don't make a mess in the kitchen. Still, Daryl "Buckshot" Fuqua just can't seem to bring himself to do what wife Wilma wants him to do. Wilma's been puttin' up with Buck's "puttin' up" for better'n 50 years now. That's what Buck calls his canning hobby, "puttin' up." What's all the fuss about? Carrots! Buck's Hot Carrots.

Buck Fuqua made a name for himself years ago. People once raved over his relish, begged for his apple butter and pined for his pear preserves. These days, Buck's settin' the woods on fire with his hot carrots. Buckshot's double-ought, two-fisted, skull and crossbones, code three and I do mean hot...carrots. See, Buck was "puttin' up" some pickles when he ran out of cucumbers. He had lots of carrots in his garden, so he started canning the little rabbit sticks, and he threw in some jalapeños to make things interesting.

Wilma swears there's something else in Buck's little welding torches, but she doesn't know exactly what that ingredient might be. He keeps the secret recipe in his head. Wilma suspects he's written it down somewhere, but Buck's not talking.

"These days Buck's settin' the woods on fire with his Hot Carrots"

Buck chops his carrots the old-fashioned way.

Somehow, word got out that Buckshot Fuqua was turning out a product, from right there in Wilma's kitchen, that would put a cowlick on a bald man. Folks started dropping by the Fuqua place to pick up some of Buck's Hot Carrots, so Buck and Wilma had to set up a distribution system. Seein' how Wal-Mart was not exactly beating down the Fuqua's door, Buckshot decided to put a few jars down at the local gas station. Since then, the number of "retail outlets" carrying the carrots has grown, and it's rumored that folks have been spotted eating Buck's Hot Carrots as far away as Piccadilly Circus in London, England, and on an Indian reservation in Arizona. One thing for sure - those carrots had to come from one of the little stores, markets or gas stations in Navasota, Texas, because that's the only place you can get them.

And that's why we're starting our tour here. If you're gonna travel Texas, you might as well take along a jar or two of Buck's Hot Carrots. If you're dyin' to have some of these little fire sticks and you can't make it to Navasota, try calling Buck and Wilma at 409-825-6315 and maybe they'll send you some.

★ BOB'S BEST BETS ★

Now we wouldn't send you that close to the birthplace of Texas without suggesting you actually see the birthplace of Texas. While you're in Navasota, it's easy to hop on down the road and across the county line to **Washington-on-the-Brazos State Historical Park** to see the **Star of the Republic Museum**. This tribute to the early beginnings of Texas is indeed star-shaped. The exhibits tell you about Texas as a nation and how Texas became a state, and there are lots of regularly scheduled living history demonstrations. The Star of the Republic Museum is open daily from 10 - 5.

The park where the museum is located contains some of the historic town site which served as the capital of the Republic of Texas from 1842 until 1846. There is also a reconstructed Independence Hall where independence from Mexico was declared. If the reconstructed building looks unfinished, that's because that's the way it was when the founding fathers met there. There is always a big celebration in the park around March 2nd, which is Texas Independence Day. This area, by the way, is usually covered in bluebonnets during the spring of the year and that, combined with the already picturesque setting on the Brazos River makes for the perfect picnic grounds.

The biggest day for the celebration is usually the Sunday closest to March 2nd, but in recent years the celebration has begun to spill over to other days as well. For more information, call 409-878-2461 to reach the museum, 409-878-2214 to reach the state park and 409-836-3695 to reach the Washington County Chamber of Commerce. The Navasota Chamber of Commerce is 409-825-6600 or 800-252-6642.

Stop and Smell the Roses

Stop #2
Independence, Texas

When I was a kid, there was a lady down the block and around the corner who spent all day long in her garden. She wore one of those old fashioned big bonnets, thick gloves and always had something that looked to me like scissors in her hand. Now my dad had a garden, but he only grew things that we considered useful like tomatoes and things we could eat. I was pretty fascinated by the lady who grew nothing but flowers...and took all day, every day, to do it.

It's been a lot of years since I was a kid and that lady tended her rose garden, but I do remember one thing very clearly: Her roses just weren't the same as the roses you get today when you order from the local florist. For the longest time I didn't understand the difference, but since we found Mike Shoup in Independence, Texas, I've come to understand that a rose is not a rose is not a rose. My neighbor was growing something called "antique roses", and you just don't see them much anymore.

Mike Shoup likes to spend his time on the bumpy backroads of Washington County looking for things like old abandoned homesteads. He thrills at the sight of an empty, falling down old whitewashed frame structure that looks like it could have been there a hundred years or better...and chills at the sight of the same structure after the bulldozers have done their job. See, Mike Shoup is a rose rustler.

Mike is looking for antique roses, and he finds them in ramshackle, old homesteads on the Texas backroads. Often, even when it appears that nothing of value could still be alive after so many years of neglect, Mike runs across the plants he calls "survivors", those that cling to life with no one to care for them but Mother Nature. In case you haven't noticed, roses from "back then" and roses from today just aren't the same. Mike says that, for some reason or another, they pretty much stopped breeding honest-to-goodness antique roses just after the Civil War. For one thing, modern day roses don't smell the same. The flower shop variety roses may look pretty, but there is something missing, and Mike makes it his job to find and preserve the roses which were lovingly planted and tended, then long ago forgotten.

Mike looks out over his Rose Emporium empire.

For Mike Shoup, thirteen years of cutting, collecting, researching and replanting have blossomed into a business. The Antique Rose Emporium is tucked away in the tiny community of Independence, just on the edge of Brenham. Located on an early settler's homestead, the eight acre retail display garden center is beautifully landscaped, featuring romantic old garden roses, native plants, old-fashioned cottage garden perennials, herbs and a wildflower meadow. Several unique restored buildings include an 1855 stone kitchen original to the site, an 1840s log corn

"Mike Shoup is a rose rustler"

15

crib, an 1850s salt box house and an early 1900s Victorian home known as Champney's Green.

The Antique Rose Emporium is not only a great place to browse and buy, it's perfect for things like weddings and receptions. Hours of operation are Monday - Saturday from 9 - 6 and Sundays from 11 - 5. If you plan to go with a large group, it's a good idea to call ahead. The Antique Rose Emporium is located 12 miles north of Brenham on FM 50 in Independence. The phone number is 409-836-5548.

★ BOB'S BEST BETS ★

While you're in the area, there are lots of other things to do around Independence and nearby Brenham. Here are a few suggestions:

Antique Carousel - This wonderful antique is one of only twelve that exist in Texas today and is the only example of a C.W. Parker Carousel with Hershell-Spillman horses. It was built sometime right after the turn of the century and is one of the few examples of a carousel built for a traveling carnival. In 1932, the citizens of Brenham got together and purchased the broken- down pieces of the carousel for the storage fee of $30! They then restored the structure and the WPA built the building it's in sometime not long after. The carousel is located in Fireman's Park at 901 N. Park. If you're alone and the carousel isn't open, you can still look inside through the plexiglass windows. Group tours of the carousel can be arranged by calling 409-277-1205.

While you're getting nostalgic about the old carousel, keep the mood alive at the **Brenham Heritage Museum**. It's in the old Federal Building, built in 1915. They're always updating the exhibits and special shows are held once or twice a year. The goal of the museum is to preserve Brenham's heritage so future generations can appreciate it years from now, but you're likely to appreciate it just as much today. The museum is located at 105 S. Market and hours are Wednesday from 1 - 4, and Thursday, Friday and Saturday from 10 - 4. Donations are appreciated.

There are two "factory tours" in Brenham worth a stop. **Ellison's Greenhouses** - they have year-round crops, but Ellison's is famous for it's 250,000 poinsettias produced every Christmas. The greenhouses are open for tours on Fridays and Saturdays and even a person traveling alone can join a tour on those days. You can arrange for group tours during the week by calling 409-836-6011. Tour admission is $2. All tours begin at the gift shop located at 1808 S. Horton. **Blue Bell Creamery** - they claim to produce about 20,000,000 gallons a year! You can tour the "little creamery in Brenham" for a nominal charge Monday through Friday by calling first 800-327-8135.

Monastery of St. Clare - 9 miles east of Brenham on Highway 105 is the home to a group of Franciscan Poor Clare Nuns. They support themselves by raising miniature horses and by selling their handmade art objects in a little gift shop. Visitors are always welcome from 2 - 4 (except Holy Week and Christmas) to drop by and pet the horses, browse the gift shop and relax in the quiet solitude of their chapel. There is a miniature horse there which appeared on the cover of our *Texas Country Reporter* newspaper and was subsequently named "Texas Country." Admission is free, but donations go to a great cause and are always welcome. Groups should call ahead for reservations and guided tour costs. 409-836-9652

Brenham has more than its share of historic homes and lots of great bed and breakfast establishments, so don't be afraid of spending a day or two in the area. The town holds an area-wide historical heritage tour early each April, a county fair in September and the annual Maifest is a tradition worth taking part in. Every business in town, even the banks, and the schools close for the big event. It's a very German festival with lots of sausage and such, an arts and crafts fair and some topnotch entertainment. Maifest is held at Austin Park north of downtown, and most of the events usually take place on Mother's Day weekend.

"They support themselves by raising miniature horses"

Symphony in the Sticks

Stop #3

Round Top, Texas

"Back in 1968, a man named James Dick strolled into Round Top with his grand piano and a peculiar idea in tow"

You might expect a little town named Round Top to be the quaintest, quietest little place around. And, for the most part, it is. But out here in the quiet of Central Texas something is causing quite a ruckus. The peaceful music of birds singing and brooks babbling has been joined by the sounds of saws sawing...and hammers hammering...and planes planing. It's been going on for three decades, and there's no end in sight.

Back in 1968, a man named James Dick strolled into Round Top with his grand piano and a peculiar idea in tow. He proposed that the fine artists and craftsmen in the area join him in creating a music hall, and not just any music hall but one of the finest in the world. The joint effort between James and the people of Round Top came to be known as Festival Hill. With blueprints existing only in James Dick's mind, this work in progress has been under construction for almost 30 years, and facilities are built only after money to pay for them is raised. It began when James raised enough money to buy six acres (Round Top's former town dump) and transformed an eyesore into what is now 200 acres of lush country gardens dotted with Victorian buildings and dominated by the concert hall. The magnificent structure on a hill near Round Top, population 81, towers above ancient live oak trees from seemingly out of nowhere. You've heard it before, but in this case it's true: You can't miss it!

James Dick's dream was not just for an incredible "work of art" building, but for an international music festival to be held there. The International Festival Institute's first concert was performed on June 4, 1976, one month before the nation's huge Bicentennial Celebration, on a rusty portable stage repainted by James Dick and his small staff. Today, students, selected in highly competitive auditions at top conservatories throughout the United States and abroad, come to Festival Hill each summer for master studies taught by a distinguished international faculty. They are members of the Texas Festival Orchestra who now perform from a stage framed by intricately carved wood paneling, most of it created by local craftsmen. James Dick's dream is alive and flourishing at Festival Hill.

Reserved tickets required for tours, but plan to experience the music, too. We think the concert tickets, at 10 bucks each, are possibly the entertainment bargain of Texas. You can get tickets at the concert hall before each concert, and, while reservations are not necessary, plan to go early to get a good seat. For a complete listing of performers and concert dates, contact Festival Hill at P.O. Drawer 89, Round Top, Texas, 78954. The e-mail address is festinst@fais.net and the phone number is 409-249-3129.

The Concert Hall as seen from the gardens

Bad news, Bob. You can only have <u>one</u> pie!

★ BOB'S BEST BETS ★

One of the great myths of the world is the one that says there are certain things you can only find in big cities. Things like culture and gourmet food. Round Top, Texas, exposes both of those myths in what some claim to be the smallest incorporated town in the state. Last time they counted that number was 81. Most big cities would dearly love to have Festival Hill in their town, and I for one would love to have **Royer's Round Top Cafe** conveniently located "just around the corner." But both of these incredible places are here in Round Top.

Bud Royer is a gourmet if ever there was one. And, yes, he used to practice his craft as a restaurant consultant. When Houston's economy spiraled down in the mid-80's, Bud found himself out of work. Then the opportunity came up to buy a restaurant in one of his favorite places. One thing lead to another and Royer's Round Top Cafe was born.

You need to know that Round Top Cafe is no hamburger and chicken-fried place, though their versions of these old standards are both wonderful. In fact, everything on the menu is wonderful. Today, that menu includes things like bread pudding with lemon sauce, salmon, fresh pasta and ribs. My personal favorites are the Mexican Pasta, Stuffed Snapper (with shrimp and crabmeat) and the Beef Tenderloin Plate with grilled onions and melted swiss cheese, horseradish dressing and onion jelly on the side. They have some wonderful yeast rolls (which they readily admit are frozen dough balls they purchase and bake - that takes nothing away from their great taste, though) and - here's the real clincher - the best pies you've ever put in your mouth. And that includes your mom's apple. The Royers offer up a chocolate chip pie that is out-of-this-world, an apple with seven fresh apples in every pie and a peach with two and a half pounds of fresh peaches in it. Everything they serve at Royer's Round Top Cafe smells good, looks good and tastes even better. No wonder people drive from all over Texas to eat in Round Top. By the way, you can order their pies through the mail by calling 1-800-624-PIES or order by FAX at 409-249-5644. You can also call the "pie" number when you're one hour away and the Royers will put your name on the waiting list. The cafe is open Wednesday through Saturday from 11 - 9 and Sunday from 12 - 4. It's a tiny place, but Bud Royer has a saying that seems to make sense: "Being small is the price you pay for ambiance."

About four miles northeast of Round Top on FM 1457 and FM 2714 is the **Winedale Historical Center** where you'll find restored ranch and farm houses, log cabins, barns and the like as a demonstration of the Anglo-German heritage of the area. Winedale is an extension of the University of Texas and there are all kinds of special events, festivals and such, or you can just drop by for a visit. The Winedale Historical Center is open for tours all day Saturdays and starting at noon on Sundays. You can tour the center by appointment only during the week. For more information, call 409-278-3530. For more information on just about anything in this area, call the Round Top Chamber of Commerce at 409-249-4042.

Michelangelo Texas-Style

Stop #4
Schulenburg, Texas

"The true artists of this incredible work were turn-of-the-century craftsmen who worked for five painstaking years"

Call us sentimental, but we appreciate the little things - a sunset over the plains, a favorite fishing hole, the lonesome spin of an out-of-work windmill. And, if you're lucky, one of those old country churches just might be around the next bend. If you're really lucky, you might get to go inside.

Along the Texas Pioneer Trail is a wonderful little town called Schulenburg - "school town" in German, though the town was actually named for a man named Schulenburg who donated the land for the depot when the GH&SA Railroad made its way to the town. Here you will find lots of historic buildings, homes and historical markers and local eating establishments which reflect the German-Czech heritage. Schulenburg is worth the trip just for those offerings, and you can find out more about the early days of the area by stopping by the Schulenburg Historical Museum at 631 North Main Street.

But the real reason we're sending you to Schulenburg is to go to church. This isn't as much for a dose of religion as it is for a dose of art. They are known as the Painted Churches, and they are famous around the world for their hand-crafted murals, frescoes and statues. To look at the ceiling in High Hill Church, you would think Michelangelo himself had somehow made it to Texas. The true artists of this incredible work were turn-of-the-century craftsmen who worked for five painstaking years.

While the churches are not all located in Schulenburg, the reason to start your visit there is so you can drop by the Chamber of Commerce to pick up a map and brochures on the painted churches in Dubina, Ammannsville, Praha and several other area communities. You can take a self-guided tour, but there is no guarantee that the churches will be unlocked. You can see quite a bit by peeking through the windows, but guided tours are available Monday - Saturday for groups of 15 or more. The chamber is located at 101-B Kessler Avenue. 409-743-4514

Talented parishioners restored the historic murals of Dubina.

★ BOB'S BEST BETS ★

No one seems to know why, (probably due to the strong German-Czech-Austrian influence) but Schulenburg is a very musical place, and just about everyone in town is in a band. Every August they hold the **Schulenburg Festival** which is three days of oom-pah and wurst mixed with a rodeo and more western events.

The nearby town of Luling started out as a railroad town filled with gunslingers, then an oil boom brought in a different type of entrepreneur, and finally a much quieter period of farming. A man named Edgar Davis made a fortune in the oil fields, then gave away a lot of the money to his employees and established the **Luling Foundation Farm**. You'll find evidence of oil's prominence in the community through a number of unique oil **pumpjack characters** in the downtown area. These working pumps are decorated with a dinosaur, a little girl picking wildflowers, a butterfly with moving wings, a pink flamingo driving a sportscar and something called a "thumpadillo." The thumpadillo probably refers to what the area is known for today - producing some fine watermelons - and the last weekend of June each year Luling hosts its three day festival called the **Watermelon Thump**.

Southeast of Luling is the town of **Gonzales**, also known as the "Lexington of Texas." Gonzales' shot may not have been heard "round the world," but it did play an important part in Texas' revolt against Mexico. The Mexican army had given the settlement a cannon to defend itself against Indian raids, then tried to take back the gift when things heated up. In 1835, the Mexican cavalry rode into Gonzales intent on retrieving the cannon. Locals raised a flag with the message "Come and take it!" They then turned the cannon on the Mexicans, driving them back to the west. Later, by the way, the citizens of Gonzales heard about the siege at the Alamo in San Antonio and sent 32 volunteers to help. All of them died at the hand of Santa Anna's troops. Today, Gonzales proudly remembers its part in Texas' independence with the **Come and Take It Festival** which is always held on the weekend closest to October 2nd, the day the first shot for independence was fired. There are the regular festival activities, and the famous battle is re-enacted. The original "Come and Take It" cannon is still on display at the local Memorial Museum and there is a Come and Take It driving tour. You can get a map and information at the local chamber at 414 St. Lawrence. 210-672-6532

In downtown Gonzales, you'll find the impressive **Gonzales County Courthouse,** famous for its Romanesque Revival design and the **Old Jail Museum**, which still sends shivers down the spine with its original gallows and cells. Be sure and ask the curator about the condemned prisoner's curse on the courthouse clocks!

Nearby **Palmetto State Park** offers an unusual variety of plant species and wildlife in a tropical setting. Be sure and ask the park ranger about the Ottine Swamp Monster. This legendary "Big Foot" type creature has been spotted by several park visitors, but his existence remains a mystery. And, speaking of Ottine, drop by the **Ottine Post Office** for a step back in time!

24

The Center of
the Domino Universe

Men like Lukas Janak have been playin' longer than they can remember. Lukas learned to count with dominoes, even practiced his ":times tables" using all those little black dots. They say Lukas was makin' downs before he was sittin' up, choosin' the spinner before he could speak. He'll tell you that if you want to domino, you better learn which rocks to cut and which rocks to turn, to get rid of your doubles, hang on to repeaters, and never, ever, down a spinner from a missing suit. Over a lifetime, Lukas, and lots of others like him here in Hallettsville, have pretty much mastered this game. That's why Hallettsville is the center of the universe when it comes to dominoes.

They say that, for domino players, it's the Superbowl, World Series and Wimbledon rolled into one. Still, knowing better than to try to compete with the Super Bowl, folks in Hallettsville host the State Championship Domino Tournament here every year on the Sunday before the Super Bowl. They come from all over the state and some from out-of-state, though real domino players don't think much of foreign competition in this game. So many people come to play in this tournament, the only place in town to hold them all is the Knights of Columbus Hall.

Unless you know your way around a domino table, we recommend visiting the tournament as a spectator, though any team can pay their 20-bucks and sign up to play. You'll have to be at least 18 unless you're playing with a relative, then ten is the minimum age. (You'll see some grandfather/grandson teams here that are pretty good!) The tournament is organized by Bob Pesek and you can get more information by calling the KC Hall at 512-798-2311. The hall is located on Highway 77 just south of Hallettsville. While you're there, don't miss the little room up front which houses the Domino Hall of Fame. Our friend Lukas Janak is there along with several other domino greats.

Stop #5

Hallettsville, Texas

"They say that, for domino players, it's the Superbowl, World Series and Wimbledon rolled into one"

Bob "sweats" a domino game at a local ice house.

★ BOB'S BEST BETS ★

While dominoes is dominant in Hallettsville, there are other activities here and nearby. The **State Championship High School Rodeo** has been held here every June for 50 years. And every April there's a big fiddle contest here called the **Fiddlers' Frolic**. There's even a **Fiddlers' Hall of Fame** in Hallettsville.

A few miles down Alt. 77 brings you to Cuero, Texas, which once was the starting place for cattle drives heading north. Today, Cuero is better known for its annual **Cuero Turkey Trot**, a festival built around the town's claim that it is the "Turkey Capital of the World." The town has a race during its festival and always enters a turkey named "Ruby Begonia" which is usually challenged by an entry from Worthington, Minnesota, which also claims to be a "Turkey Capital."

Three miles south of town on the Guadalupe River is what remains of Clinton, Texas, once the site of an ongoing family feud that rivals the legend of the Hatfields and McCoys. Seems two members of the Taylor family were killed in the late 1860s, followed by retaliatory slayings of the Sutton family. The feud went on for at least ten years. Today, there is little left of Clinton.

The Aggie Bootmaker

The noise erupts like a volcano high above the Brazos River. It's game day in College Station, home to one of the greatest traditions in the country, and students and alums alike come to cheer on their beloved team, the fightin' Aggies. And at the center of the madness is the famous Texas A & M Corps of Cadets. The Corps is the spirit of this university, the tradition keepers, the personification of all things Aggie. Set off by the uniform, the gloves, the saber, you can see the honor in their eyes. But the most sacred possession of all Aggie cadets is the boots. Nothing means more to a senior Corps member than his boots.

Just a few blocks away from the A & M campus, almost in the shadow of the famous Kyle Field, in a simple, storefront shop, Johnny Holick spent a lifetime building boots for Aggies. In fact, if you see a senior Aggie Corps member, Johnny Holick made his boots. He has since the days when Herbert Hoover was president. He first shod the class of 1932. Since then, he estimates he's made at least 60,000 pair of Aggie boots. But even in '32, the Holick boot business was not new. Johnny's daddy had been in the boot business since 1891, cowboy boots mostly, and the shop was first tucked away in the corner of Joseph Holick's Aggie dorm room. In fact, it was Joseph Holick who first pulled together a handful of musicians to march together in time. Today, that group, once led by an Austrian clarinet player, is known as the Aggie Band. Johnny Holick followed in his father's musical footsteps, too, and once made his living playing the piccolo on silent movie sound tracks. Then, when the "talkies" put him out of business during the Great Depression, young Johnny found a way to make money by making the cadet boots.

Johnny says he learned some of the boot business from his dad, but Joseph was just a "bottomer" when he started as a cobbler in Austria... he had no idea how to make the top part of the boot, so he couldn't teach that to his son. Johnny picked that up on his own.

Stop #6

College Station, Texas

"He first shod the class of 1932. Since then, he estimates he's made at least 60,000 pair of Aggie boots"

The Aggie Bootmaker's shop is always busy.

Then, in more recent years, he taught all he knows to several other "boot artists" so they can carry on the tradition. Johnny figures 90 years old is a good time to retire, so he's rarely at the shop these days. But the Aggie boots are still made right there in Holick's. But you can still drop by the shop at 106 College Main in College Station and see where the famous Aggie boots are made. And, if you're lucky, perhaps Johnny Holick himself will drop by to check in while you're there. The phone number at Holick's is 409-846-6721.

★ BOB'S BEST BETS ★

College Station and its nearby sister city, **Bryan**, may look landlocked on the map, but there's a port here you should visit. There's also a good white and an outstanding red. Of course, we're talking wine, not boats, and the place is the **Messina Hof** winery in Bryan.

Actually, they joke that at Messina Hof they only make white and maroon wine, in keeping with the Aggie colors. Whatever the color, Messina Hof has won some impressive international awards for its port, cabernet sauvignon and merlot. You'll find the label is served in many top restaurants in and out of Texas.

Tours of the winery include a visit to the vineyards and you'll see a mechanical grape crusher and a bottling machine from Italy which appears to be on its last leg and is literally held together by duct tape and baling wire. If you really want to experience the wine business, visitors can even sign up to help pick the grapes during harvest season. There is a restaurant on-site, and a bed and breakfast for those who can't get enough of the winery with a short visit.

Messina Hof is located east of Texas Highway 6 at 4545 Old Reliance Road. Tours are given at 1:00 and 2:30 weekdays, 11:00, 12:30, 2:30 and 4:00 on Saturdays and at 12:30 and 2:30 on Sundays. For more information, call 409-778-9463.

If you missed Royer's Round Top Cafe during your visit to Festival Hill, be sure to stop by Bud Royer's new restaurant in College Station! It's located at 2500 S. Texas Avenue and is open Tuesday - Thursday, and Sunday 11-10; Friday and Saturday 11-11. 409-694-8826 or 888-881-PIES

Opening in College Station in November 1997 is the **George Bush Presidential Library and Museum**. It will be the tenth presidential library administered by the National Archives and its holdings will include 36 million pages of official and personal papers and 40,000 artifacts that document President Bush's long public career. Though not complete at this writing, President Bush has promised you will find documentation for some of the most revolutionary changes that the world has ever seen take place. That would include things like the peace talks, the unification of Germany, the decline and fall of the Soviet Union and Desert Storm. The library and museum will be on the West Campus of Texas A & M University.

Marlin's Medical Miracle?

"People who grew up in Marlin in those days will tell you that the mineral water was as much a part of life as Friday night football games and farm reports"

It begins far below the streets of Marlin, in wells the size of oceans. Minerals and water mix together in some cosmic concoction, then the steaming recipe flows up and out the only remaining release, a marble fountain in downtown Marlin. It never stops. The water flows from that fountain all day, every day, and some people still think it has magical healing powers. Back in 1893, when Marlin was known as Bucksnort, a man named Wiley Clark stopped to bathe in a Marlin ditch. After that roadside dip, old Wiley told folks his skin problems had miraculously cured themselves - or, Wiley wondered, could it be the water? Seems someone drilling for just plain old water struck a hot mineral well. Word spread, and the story of Marlin's medical miracle flowed like, well, like water from a well.

People who grew up in Marlin in those days will tell you that the mineral water was as much a part of life as Friday night football games and farm reports. Over the years, they've seen it "cure" everything from arthritis to indigestion. For four decades or so, the world beat a path to Marlin's door, with people making annual pilgrimages just to take a bath. The entire New York Giants team used to travel to Texas to partake in Marlin's magical mystery. No one seemed to know how it worked, and lots of folks doubted if it worked, but folks still came. Until modern medicine made things like healing waters seem to be a lot of hocus-pocus. Then the big cars and the sports teams and the hotels and hospitals all pulled out, leaving Marlin and her weird water behind.

Today, as homeopathy seems to be finding its place alongside modern medicine, Marlin's mineral water is finding a place with believers once again. Folks are starting to drop by for a drink or a bucket of the water, and at least one man of science, Dr. David Fedro, is prescribing a relaxing, therapeutic bath in the whirlpools he has built in Marlin. David doesn't claim the water is a cure-all, but he does think there is room for alternative medicine accompanied by a healthy dose of positive attitude in most people's lives today. That, he says, is the kind of thing you just might get from the water in Marlin.

Marlin during her heyday

Marlin Mineral Water can be had for free at the Hot Water Pavilion in downtown Marlin at 245 Coleman. Baths are available through the Brazos Rehab Center. The Marlin chamber can provide more information by contacting them at 254-883-2171.

★ BOB'S BEST BETS ★

Just south of Marlin is the tiny town of **Rosebud**. For years, folks there have made the claim that every home in Rosebud has at least one rose bush. Drive through and see for yourself on your way to **Cameron**. That's where you can see the city in miniature. Our old friend John Johnson built the recreation of Cameron in the 30s from his boyhood memories. He wanted Cameron to be remembered the way he remembered it, so he built it in his garage in Austin, then transported it to Cameron where it is on display at Main Street Market Antique Mall at 104 W. Main.

Just What the Doctor Ordered

Stop #8

Waco, Texas

"After two years of testing, blending and processing, the new flavor was perfected and put on sale "

Funny how things we are so familiar with got their start. I have a friend who started a large chain of restaurants in his mother-in-law's kitchen in Abilene. I once did a story on a fellow who was making hot sauce in his kitchen just to give away to his friends and family. A year or two after we aired the story on his little business, he sold it to a huge conglomerate! And then there's the story of the humble beginnings of one of Texas' "native son" trademarks.

Dr Pepper got its start as a fountain drink mixed in the Old Corner Drug Store in Waco, Texas, in the 1880s. R.S. Lazenby was a beverage chemist and patron of the drug store when he became interested in the new drink that had been invented by a pharmacist there and began extensive research. He later purchased the pharmacy and its new soft drink formula. After two years of testing, blending and processing, the new flavor was perfected and put on sale commercially. Even then, Dr Pepper was a minor player in the industry, with Lazenby's Circle "A" Ginger Ale outselling it in the early days ten-to-one! But Dr Pepper caught on and Lazenby's work was so good, the Dr Pepper formula has changed very little over the years. Today, Dr Pepper/7 Up Corporation is one of the giants of the soft drink industry. The headquarters moved to Dallas many years ago, but the original corporate location and bottling plant still stands in Waco. In fact, it is the only original soft drink plant (among the big soft drink companies) which still stands today. The building is on the National Historic Register of Historic Places.

They don't make Dr Pepper at the original plant in Waco anymore, but they have preserved the location as a museum dedicated to not only the Dr Pepper brand, but to the entire soft drink industry. A restored operating soda fountain is located on the ground floor and you can still get a Dr Pepper there that is actually mixed by the server using a combination of DP "formula" and carbonated soda water. In the back of the first floor there is an antique bottling machine, one of the inventions which catapulted the soft drink industry into the important part of society it occupies today.

From Dr Pepper to free enterprise, it's all here!

The Dr Pepper Museum isn't just about the soft drink industry. Longtime company chairman W.W. "Foots" Clements is a big believer in American free enterprise, so the third floor of the museum also houses the Clements Free Enterprise Institute where visitors can see a topnotch video presentation which was produced as a tribute to Dr Pepper, the soft drink industry and free enterprise. The video is aimed at the thousands of young visitors the museum receives every year, but it should be enjoyable to just about anyone.

The Dr Pepper Museum is located at 300 S. 5th Street. There is a small admission fee. Call 254-757-1024 for more information.

The look may change, but the taste stays the same

★ BOB'S BEST BETS ★

There is so much to see and do in Waco, we'll list only a few and leave it to you to explore this Brazos River town to see what you can find on your own. They say Waco grew, survived and still exists today on the "5 Cs": cattle, cotton, corn, collegians and culture. A Texas Ranger fort was built here in 1837, and today, the **Texas Ranger Hall of Fame and Museum** at Fort Fisher is one of the premier attractions in this town. There is a famous collection of guns and weapons from the Old West, lots of Indian artifacts and western art. Displays commemorate the history and heritage of the Texas Rangers. It is open daily from 9 - 5 and there is a charge for admission. 254-750-8631

At one time the old suspension bridge which crosses

the Brazos in Waco was the nation's largest suspension bridge. The Chisholm Trail passed over this bridge and the famous Brooklyn Bridge in New York was later patterned after it. Today, you can still walk across the old suspension bridge.

Another Waco template for the way things will one day be is the 51 acre natural habitat **Cameron Park Zoo**. This is a beautiful setting near the Brazos River, where animals live amid pecan, elm, live oak, burr oak, cottonwood, bamboo and mesquite trees. Everytime I visit there, I come away thinking that if I were a wild animal, I might like to live there. The zoo has recreational and educational exhibits. The Cameron Park Zoo is home to monkeys, Sunatran tigers, white rhinos, giraffes, zebras, antelopes and other species. The new reptile center has a very special resident: an Iguana named "Bob" after some television guy who donated him to the zoo. Bob gets to live during the winter in a special window habitat in the zoo's gift shop and loves for visitors to drop by and say, "Hi." Located at 1701 N. 4th St. and open Monday - Saturday 9 -5, Sunday 11 - 5.

One of the often overlooked attractions in Waco is the **Governor Bill and Vara Daniel Historic Village**. Along the shaded banks of the Brazos River sit more than 20 wood-frame buildings which represent a Texas farming community in the 1890s. The 13-acre site includes a cotton gin, blacksmith shop, livery stable, hotel, saloon, church, school and the homes of landlord, sharecropper and tenant farmers. The site is open throughout the year and offers a look back at rural life in Texas. For more information, call 254-755-1160. Admission is $3 for adults, $2 dollars for seniors and $1 for students.

If you're a domino player or know someone who is, the only domino factory outside China is located in nearby Clifton, Texas, and they have a factory store in Waco. **Puremco,** Inc., makes all kinds of dominoes and can even personalize a set for you. They sell seconds, too, at quite a savings. 5002 S. Loop 340, Waco, 76706. 254-662-6084

Come Clean
with Goat Milk Soap

Stop #9
Hamilton, Texas

Arvil Boatner admits that it's some of the worst smelling stuff on the face of the earth. So how come he wants to sell it to you to use in your bath or shower? We're talking soap here. Goat milk soap. "Nanny's Best," to be specific.

Arvil and Sharon Boatner say thanks to them and a few others, Hamilton County is the number one producer of goat milk soap in the state. Not that other counties are plotting ways to knock them off that lofty perch. In fact, few others in all of Texas seem to be taken with goat milk soap quite like the Boatners.

They started with a few goats, a kitchen and an old Hamilton Beach mixer. Today they produce 170 pounds of soap every day. And that's just to keep up with the demand. The recipe they use is more than 100 years old, and one of the most popular varieties is their "Goat Milk Soap on a Rope," which resembles an off

Arvil keeps his herd happy.

white cow patty. But even with the foul smell during the "cooking" process and the similarities to barnyard relics, goat milk soap is a hit. People who use it say it works great and it's good for your skin.

That doesn't stop Arvil and Sharon from hearing frequently asked questions like "Will I eat tin cans after using this?" or "Will this make me smell like a goat?" And for every question there is an answer. In this case it's usually "Not if you didn't do those things before!"

You can find goat milk soap (and the Boatners' new prickly pear cactus products) at their goat farm. From Hamilton take FM 932 approximately 8 miles. Take a right on FM 3340. Take a left on County Road 409 for 7/10 of a mile and you'll see the sign. You can call the Boatners to order their products at 800-687-GOAT.

★ BOB'S BEST BETS ★

There is a **Hamilton County Museum** located inside the courthouse on the square in Hamilton. If you're up for the out-of-the-ordinary and you don't mind loud noises, schedule your visit to Hamilton on November 11th. That's Armistice Day, the day that World War I ended back in 1919. The event was celebrated across the country with something called an **"Anvil Shoot,"** and darned if the folks in Hamilton don't still shoot the anvil every year in commemoration. What they do is fill a large anvil with black powder, place another anvil on top and draw a red hot metal rod along the point that they meet. The result is a noise that would wake the dead... and often the living. You see, this whole ceremony takes place at 4:00 AM. That's right, four o'clock in the morning. Why? Because it's 11:00 PM Versailles time! The event wraps up with a good breakfast for all. It's held at the American Legion Hall on US 281 just north of town. 254-386-5450

Not far away is Clifton, which was established by Norwegian settlers, and today you can see the beauty of the land by taking a **Norse Country Tour**. 254-386-3216

"But even with the foul smell during the cooking process and the similarities to barnyard relics, goat milk soap is a hit"

Even The King
Played Cherry Spring

Stop #10
Cherry Spring, Texas

"Then, one day, everything changed. Music came to Cherry Spring"

You've heard of "blink and you'll miss it" towns. Well, let me tell you, you could be wide awake, use a map, have a friend tell you to look and still miss Cherry Spring. The one and only building in Cherry Spring was originally built in 1890 by a one-time Apache captive named Herman Lehmann. For years, it served the neighboring ranches as saloon, post office and general dry goods store rolled into one. Then, one day, everything changed. Music came to Cherry Spring. Now, I'm not sure why, but there are lots of places in this vicinity of Texas like the Cherry Springs Dance Hall. The most famous of them, Luckenbach, is not that far away. But for all the folks who played those other places, there were ten more who played Cherry Spring. Time was, anybody who was anybody in country music played the Cherry Springs Dance Hall. They used to get touring acts from the Louisiana Hayride and the Grand Ole Opry. Patsy Cline played here. Hank Williams played here. Bob Wills and Ernest Tubb played here. And, before you ask, yes "The King" played here, too. Newspaper ads and posters say Elvis played Cherry Spring on October 9, 1955. The ticket price? A whopping buck-fifty!

All the greats were here. That is, until country music changed. The big names started filling concert arenas instead of dance halls, and places like Cherry Springs Dance Hall lost out to sheer numbers which translated to sheer dollars. So, not long ago, after a hundred years of history and harmony, they shut her down. Cherry Springs was quiet once again. The old building was a cedar yard and a hay barn and just kind of fell apart. But, today, Cherry Springs is open again. We don't know if this will last forever, so you better visit soon just in case.

At Cherry Springs Dance Hall, they play both kinds of music — country and western. And folks don't come out just to toe-tap. They're here to dance the Texas

Blink and you may miss Cherry Springs.

Two-Step and the Schottische, even a cowboy's version of the Mexican Hat Dance. At Cherry Springs Dance Hall, they'll dance to just about anything that has a beat. Note that I said "just about" anything. There is one rule: no line dances. The only line you'll find here is the one outside the ladies room. One local cowboy told us that, in his opinion, no one can line dance and look good doing it!

These days, lots of up and coming country music stars can be seen first at Cherry Springs. It's come to be kind of a proving ground for the pre-Nashville set, a good place to find out what audiences like and what they don't like. And it's a good place to go to hear some great entertainment in a great atmosphere. By the way, the town is named Cherry Spring, but the dance hall is Cherry Springs. Why? They just thought it sounded better!

Cherry Spring is located on Highway 87, 16 miles north of Fredericksburg. There is usually a dance on Saturday night, but not always. For that reason, call first before driving a long distance. 830-669-2580. Admission is $6 for adults, 12 and under are free, and, yes, it is a family atmosphere where it should be okay to take the kids.

★ BOB'S BEST BETS ★

While you're in the area, you'll want to travel north up 87 to **Mason**. This is the only place in North America where you can find Topaz, the state stone. In fact, most of the semi-precious stones are found in creek beds on one of two ranches, and a couple of the locals have even learned how to cut and polish the stones. You may have seen the **Star of Texas Topaz** stones. Well, this is where they come from and where that particular cut got its start. Mason has a great town square with an old courthouse in the middle. Go into just about any store on the square and they will either sell you a topaz or tell you where you can get it. Be careful: rumor has it that the stones have become so popular that some Brazilian Topaz is sneaking into the dwindling Topaz supply...not that there is anything wrong with Brazilian Topaz, it's just that any real Texan will surely want the real Texas gem.

Travel south on Highway 87 from Cherry Springs and you'll find yourself in **Fredericksburg**. This is the Santa Fe of Texas. While the huge popularity of the town and surrounding area have pumped lots of money into the local economy and brought about more and more great places to shop, some folks claim the commercialism has taken something away from the charming atmosphere. We don't think so. It's true that some of the stores are just small town versions of big city establishments (in fact, some are actually owned by merchants from Dallas, San Antonio and Houston), but the quaint German atmosphere prevails in Fredericksburg, and you can still find the small, ethnic, Hill Country town which has been there all along. And you can still find unique people and places that you can't find anywhere else.

Roy Bellows is just the kind of personality we're talking about. Roy has a blacksmith shop in his backyard. (Isn't that great? Bellows? Blacksmith?) But in truth it's located in another century. He forges imagination and hard steel further into the past, to a time when the village blacksmith was part craftsman, part magician. Roy is a little of both, and he has a special way of teasing and twisting metal. He's also about the only blacksmith in Texas who has never put shoes on a horse. He says he wouldn't even know which end to start from, but when it comes to artwork, Roy Bellows is a thoroughbred. He says that in the world of hi-tech everything what we really need is hi-touch. So, in Roy's shop you'll find functional art, the kind of things you just can't buy out of a catalog. The real treat to come from a visit to Roy's shop though, is the profound thought pouring from the man himself. It's hard to explain here, but suffice it to say - perhaps warn to the squeamish - that a visit to Roy Bellows' blacksmith shop will challenge your beliefs and maybe even shake your world!

"Roy Bellows' blacksmith shop will challenge your beliefs and maybe even shake your world!"

Roy Bellows' Blacksmith Shop is located behind his house at 507 E. Schubert. Roy asks that you call 830-997-7806 before a visit, but you can see examples of his work at a place just across the street called **Old Mill Settlement**. This bed and breakfast offers 15 restored log cabins from all over the country.

Another place worthy of a visit in Fredericksburg is the **Bauer Toy Museum**. Remember that little metal pedal car you had (or wanted) as a kid? It's here. So are toy soldiers, fire trucks, airplane replicas and lots of toys from bygone days. There is also a hand-crafted village with toy cars and trains and a 35-foot-long diorama depicting Charles Dickens' "A Christmas Carol." The toy museum is located at 233 Main Street and is open weekdays and Sundays 1 - 4:30, Saturdays 10 - 5. Donations are appreciated.

A Lone Star Stonehenge

If you haven't noticed yet, we're not much for the hurry, hustle and headaches of the big city. We like the slow lane, the backroad. And we like everyday folks who do everyday things. Folks like Doug Hill of Hunt, Texas. Doug is a tile and masonry contractor. He likes to work with rocks, too, creating artistic things that are a little bit different. Yep, Doug is a common, everyday kinda guy and you can usually find him doing common, everyday kinds of things, like plastering a wall, putting in some floor tiles...or building a replica of a 4,000-year-old sculpture.

He calls it Stonehenge and there's a reason for that. Right there in the countryside near Hunt stands a replica of the famous ruins. Located in southern England, Stonehenge is a monument to mystery. Huge stones over 12-feet high, weighing more than four tons each, were erected and arranged in a 94-foot circle with five arches inside. Theories on the purpose of

Stonehenge in the Hill Country?

Stonehenge range from royal palace to ancient calendar to extra-terrestrial involvement. No one is exactly sure why there is a Stonehenge in England. But in Hunt, Texas, they've got a pretty good idea. Doug Hill.

Doug says he built Stonehenge II (our name, not Doug's) just because he thought it would look good. And because it's something that no one else has. He's got that right. Most people do not have a sculpture the size of a house in front of their house. It takes a special individual to start with a rock and end up with a replica of Stonehenge. Doug is that special guy.

You can find Stonehenge II on FM 1340 about two miles west of Hunt.

★ BOB'S BEST BETS ★

The area in and around Hunt, Texas, is one of the prettiest spots in the state and it's well worth the time spent to just drive the backroads and explore. If you like arts and crafts, antiques and quaint little shops, stop in at nearby **Ingram** for a visit. If you're more into nature, try one of the local swimming holes on the headwaters of the Guadalupe River.

Just a few short miles from Hunt is the legendary town of **Kerrville**. This place is easily the festival capital of the Hill Country with the famous Kerrville Folk Festival, the Wine and Music Festival, the Texas Heritage Music Festival, the Texas State Arts & Crafts Fair, the Southwest Regional Kerrville EAA Fly-In, The Senior Games and the Easter Weekend Activities all taking place here. Kerrville is also a major Hill Country cultural center with the Hill Country Museum, the Hill Country Arts Foundation and the world famous **Cowboy Artists of America Museum** located here. The CAA comprises the nation's most distinguished living artists who follow in the tradition of Russell and Remington in celebrating the Old West in art. It is open Monday - Saturday 9 - 5 and Sundays 1 - 5. Adult admission is $2.50, one of the best museum deals anywhere. For more information on Kerrville call 800-221-7958.

If you're looking for Vermont-like autumn color, nearby **Lost Maples State Natural Area** is the best fall color viewing in the state. It's about one and a half hours southwest of Kerrville and the 2,174 acre park has the state's only maple forest. There are lots of picnic and camp sites, restrooms with showers and hiking trails. Call 830-966-3413 for reservations and information.

"It takes a special individual to start with a rock and end up with a replica of Stonehenge"

A Big Band in Boerne

Stop #12

Boerne, Texas

Remember the movie "The Music Man" in which Robert Preston plays the part of Professor Harold Hill, a somewhat unethical salesman who convinces the people of River City that they need a town band? His motive was to sell band instruments with the promise of forming a band and teaching the town's kids to march and play. Well, I remember the first time I heard about the Boerne Village Band, I pictured something like that movie, with the town's young people barely playing instruments while they barely marched along. Was I ever wrong!

First, the Boerne Village Band isn't kids at all, though there are some young members. Second, members of this band can really entertain folks. In fact, some people in Boerne grow up aspiring to join the band, so they take it very seriously. The band started almost 140 years ago. At times the band has had several dozen members, but today they number 17

The music never ends in Boerne.

- 20. At this writing, Dr. Kenneth Herbst is the leader of the group, though that is something which is passed on from one generation to the next.

One of the fascinating things about the Boerne Village Band is the members. Back ten or so years ago when we were visiting with the band to produce a television story about them, I remember meeting two men who had actually fought against one another during World War II. One member fought with the American forces. The other with the German forces. After the war, the German soldier eventually immigrated to the United States where he settled in Boerne, a very German community, and joined the Boerne Village Band. The two members recounted a story where they realized they were both in the same battle at the same time. Forty years later, they sat side-by-side as members of the band. Another story which made an impression on me was that of father-son members. Obviously, the band is about a lot more than just music, but their music is wonderful!

You can listen to the Boerne Village Band by visiting Boerne during June and July. During the summer months, the band performs at the gazebo downtown on the square every other Tuesday night, usually for about two hours starting at 7:30. The first thing you'll notice is that few folks just sit and listen. This is a true "oom-pah" band, though their selections include more than just traditional German folk music. To find out an exact schedule of performances, call 830-249-8000. The concerts are free, but donations are appreciated.

"One of the fascinating things about the Boerne Village Band is the members"

★ BOB'S BEST BETS ★

Boerne is a beautiful little Hill Country town well worth a visit. There are over 140 historic structures here to go along with the deep respect for the town's cultural and ancestral past. Spend an afternoon visiting the town's shops, relaxing at the nationally acclaimed **Cibolo Wilderness Trail**, an inner city greenbelt with nature center, boardwalk and walking trails, or just chatting with the colorful local residents. Behind City

Hall is the **Kuhlmann-King Historical Home** where docents, often in period costume, describe the way early settlers lived and offer tours of this graceful stone house.

Also near Boerne is the **Cave Without A Name**. There's not another cave in Texas quite like this one. Cave owner Eugene Ebell's house sits right on top of the cave. Eugene himself will be happy to take you down a narrow stairway to see the cave for the very reasonable cost of just 5-bucks. What you'll see is one of the largest caves in the Hill Country, a living cave with a creek running through it, and you'll hear Eugene Ebell's explanation of all the cave's characteristics. You can find the Cave Without A Name on State Highway 474 about 13 miles outside Boerne. Watch for the direction signs on the side of the road. The Cave Without A Name is only open when Eugene Ebell wants it to be open, so you better call first. 830-537-4212

Traveling from Boerne toward Kerrville, stop by **Welfare**, a very wide spot in the road where you should visit **PoPo's Restaurant**, located in an interesting limestone building with a beer garden. This is where the locals go for fried chicken, catfish and great desserts. Hundreds, maybe even thousands, of commemorative plates line the walls of PoPo's. Then make your way to Comfort, another beautiful little German town with lots of great shops and restaurants.

The town of **Comfort** was named for its picturesque site in 1854, and the name still holds true today. Much of the midtown area is on the National Register of Historic Places, and a 1930 art deco theater frequently hosts stage plays. But one of the most interesting places is the **"Treue der Union"** monument located near the high school. It recalls the town's Civil War hostilities between Confederate forces and the Union-sympathetic Germans. Some 65 residents fled the area, only to be ambushed by Confederates on the Nueces River in 1863. 19 settlers were killed. The monument is the only one dedicated to the Union south of the Mason-Dixon line.

Something Fishy on Television

When you sit down to watch television with Larry Piltz, you kind of get the feeling that it's not the TV he's watching. You get the feeling that Larry's off on some other plane. You get the feeling there's something fishy going on.

Larry Piltz was at his grandmother's garage sale when he noticed this huge RCA Color Deluxe set he'd grown up watching was on the floor. Being the sentimental type about things like this, Larry couldn't stand to see the old set with the green picture go, so he decided to give it new life. He decided to take television in a whole new direction, at least in his life. He decided to create and maintain new life within the

Stop #13

Austin, Texas

Larry gives an old TV new life.

former confines of a household appliance. Larry removed the picture tube from the old television cabinet and installed an aquarium in its place. Now there are Larry Piltz television aquariums all over Austin, Texas, not just in Larry's home where he has several, but in places like Esther's Follies Theater where there are seven aquariums. And Larry has taken his TV aquariums a step further, installing them in things like old stand up radios and in video arcade games. In doing so, he just may have improved radio and television!

Larry admits that he and his creations are a bit weird, but each piece is a 3D journey where Larry claims art meets ecology, antique meets kick, multimedia informs design, and vintage begats invention. Huh? Well, those are Larry's words, not ours.

Larry has a new studio where he creates his functional art pieces. There's a great overlook of Austin from his place in central West Austin, up the road from Mt. Bonnell. If you'd like to drop by, he only asks that you call ahead first to 512-452-1717. He has lots of examples of his aquariums along with several works-in-progress.

"He decided to create and maintain new life within the former confines of a household appliance"

★ BOB'S BEST BETS ★

There's so much to do in Austin that it's hard to know where to start. The capitol has undergone an extensive renovation and is well worth the tour. The Texas State Cemetery is, too. The town adopted the slogan **"Live Music Capital of the World"** and constantly lives up to that name at venues all over town, especially on the famous 6th Street. Also, there are places like **The Broken Spoke** on South Lamar, a honky tonk where country music legends can be seen and heard regularly, and **Antone's** where blues legends like Muddy Waters and Buddy Guy have played. There is more going on in Austin than any other Texas city, and you can find out the things that interest you by calling the Austin Convention and

Visitors Bureau at 512-474-5171 or 800-926-2282 or by visiting them at 201 E. 2nd Street. If you're in a hurry, visit the Austin CVB web site at www.austintexas.org.

We, of course, are always on the lookout for unusual things to do, and there are more of those in Austin, too. One recommendation would have to include a return to the Age of Steam via a trip on the **Hill Country Flyer**. Some folks created a new railroad called the Austin and Texas Central and rescued an old steam engine from a park where she had set idle for three decades. Today, the Hill Country Flyer is proudly pulled by Old Number 786. The trip goes from the Austin area to Burnet and back. It leaves Cedar Park, an Austin suburb, each Saturday and Sunday at 10 with a return at 5:30. Call 512-477-8468 for reservations and ticket costs.

Another unique Austin adventure calls for a trip to 49th and Sinclair and the Rosedale neighborhood of Austin, where Mike and Karen Collins bought the ugliest house on the block. People wondered why they wanted the old wreck, but Mike and Karen are experts on old houses, and they made an amazing discovery. Under the siding and odd boards was a log cabin built in 1847. At the time, Austin was miles away and the log home was the center of a 4,000 acre farmstead, but eventually it was carved down to two small residential lots as the approaching city gave way to neighborhoods instead of farm animals. The old log house, it seems, survived only because the previous owners were too poor to tear it down, so they just built around, and over it. Needless to say, archeologists have descended on the find and have dug up metal arrow points, bottles, muzzle-loading rifle parts and two Republic of Texas buttons. What's happened since the Collins discovery is the emergence of a reconstructed authentic mid-1800s log house. A historical marker now stands outside the cabin at 4811 Sinclair Avenue. Mike and Karen have an "open house" each spring, but otherwise tours are offered only once a month. Admission is free, but you need to call ahead to schedule a visit. 512-323-2470

Don't Sit Here!

Stop #14

San Antonio, Texas

Barney Smith remembers the days that when "nature called," he had to grab the kerosene lantern and Sears catalog and head outside right in the middle of a Texas blue norther. It was just a part of life, but pipes, pliers and plumbers changed all that. When Barney was knee high to a monkey wrench he started sticking his head under people's sinks. After a lifetime of plumbing practice and a warehouse of memories, Barney Smith's legacy is a lifetime of lids.

Barney Smith has decorated and dedicated about 400 toilet seat lids, artistically altering the functional commode covers to become hanging history. And he has generously hung them for the world to see... right there in his garage. Welcome to Barney Smith's Toilet Seat Museum!

Barney says folks often wonder if he's got all his marbles. He says he definitely has all his marbles and lots of knives, forks and spoons washed down South Texas drains, along with some unmentionables too. Lots of times Barney found himself taking out toilets to

Barney shows off his lifetime of lids

replace them with newer versions. When that happened, Barney was not bashful about asking for one special part - the toilet seat. Then he would decorate each seat with something special, things like keepsakes from a special vacation or mementos from an historic moment. Barney will settle for just about any item as long as it will fit on a toilet seat. And as long as folks don't mind it being displayed in his Toilet Seat Museum.

Barney's museum is at 239 Abiso Avenue. Before a visit, call 210-824-7791. Admission is free.

★ BOB'S BEST BETS ★

Now you might think that if we were going to suggest a tour of a shoe company in Texas that it would have to be a boot factory. Not so, though that, too, is a good idea. You know those sensible, no-nonsense shoes you should be wearing on just about any walking tour? They're made right here in San Antonio at the SAS factory. What does SAS stand for? Well, **San Antonio Shoes**, of course!

Visit SAS and you can watch the shoe leather being cut and glued. And, yes, they do make boots at SAS and you can go through that part of the factory too. Their boots sell from $450 to $4000 and their custom orders take up to eight months to get. In front of the factory is a general store where you can eat cookies and peanuts and drink fresh lemonade while you shop for seconds from the factory.

The SAS factory is located at 101 New Laredo Highway in southwest San Antonio. Tours are Monday through Friday at 10:15, 12:30 and 2:15 and include a free key chain! Call 210-924-6562.

Downtown San Antonio is, of course, filled with many wonderful tourist attractions such as the Alamo and Riverwalk, so a lot of folks naturally miss a pretty neat place right in the middle of it all. It's the **Hertzberg Circus Museum** which holds big top memorabilia such as Mr. and Mrs. Tom Thumb's carriages, old costumes, photographs, circus posters, and an entire circus in miniature. Open daily except

"Barney will settle for just about any item as long as it will fit on a toilet seat"

Sunday 10 - 5. Sundays Noon - 5. Admission fee. 210 W. Market Street. 210-207-7810

Meet the people who made Texas the rich and varied state it is today at the **Institute of Texan Cultures**. 26 ethnic and cultural groups are featured in exhibits detailing countries of origin, lifestyles, food, clothing, music, and festivals. The highlight of a visit is the dramatic multimedia presentation on 36 screens set into the domed ceiling of the foyer. In August, many visitors brave the South Texas heat to participate in the

Folklife Festival dancers demonstrate the art of Ballet Folklorico.

Texas Folklife Festival in which folks demonstrate their fascinating ways of life to the public. The Institute is located at 801 South Bowie Street and is open Tuesday through Sunday, 9 - 5. Admission fee. 2 hours free parking with admission ticket. 210-458-2300

Just east of San Antonio, about 30 miles down I-10, is the town of Seguin. If you're interested in things of an extra-terrestrial nature, you'd do well to visit **MUFON** headquarters there. MUFON, of course, stands for Mutual UFO Network. It was started by a man named Walter Andrus who claims to have witnessed a UFO in 1948. That sighting, it seems, changed his life and he has since dedicated it to finding out what's "out there." MUFON is located at 628 N. Hwy. 123 Bypass. They have a huge number of files on UFO sightings and experiences, including lots of pictures of what they claim are UFOs. Call 210-379-9216 for more information including hours. Admission is free. Donations are appreciated.

While in San Antonio, be sure to take a walk down the streets some call the most beautiful in Texas. They're in the **King William Historic District**, an area settled by prominent German merchants. Many of the Victorian homes are still in use, while others are under restoration. The **Steves Homestead** at 509 King William Street, however, is open to the public. Visitors can see the elegant 1870s-era furnishings inside daily 10 - 4:15. Admission fee. Walking tour maps are available from the King William Association office at 1032 S. Alamo. They're open Tuesday through Saturday, 10 - 2. If they're closed, look for brochures on the porch.

For generations, a favorite spot for families has been beautiful **Brackenridge Park**. It's got something for everyone with a playground, golf course, and riding stables. The **Japanese Tea Garden** is an oasis of tranquility in the middle of the bustling city, offering rustic stone bridges, winding walkways, and gleaming pools. First-time visitors can get oriented with a ride on the open-air sky-ride. This peaceful trip ends at the **San Antonio Zoo**, home of the continent's third largest animal collection. If you're afraid of heights, see the sights by rail with a ride on the **Brackenridge Eagle Miniature Train**.

Brackenridge Park is located at 3800 Broadway and is open 24 hours. Free admission. 210-821-3000. The zoo is open daily 9:30 - 5 (until 6:30 April - November). Admission fee. 210-734-7183. The stables are open Monday through Friday, 8:30 - 3; weekends, 9 - 4. Call 210-732-8881 for rates. The sky-ride and train operate weekdays 10 - 5 and weekends 9:30 - 7. 210-734-7183

Father Bird in the Valley of the Parrots

Stop #15

The Rio Grande Valley, Texas

The Rio Grande Valley is a place abundant with colorful people and things to do, but nothing is as colorful as the Wild Birds of the Valley. Father Tom Pincelli, known in these parts as Father Bird, is at the center of the wild birding universe from his church in La Feria. Seems the valley is covered with wild parrots and parakeets, all kinds of tropical birds which, for some reason or other, now live in the trees and towers of South Texas. Father Bird operates a bird hotline with a recorded message that's updated frequently with information on the latest bird sightings in the valley. The Rare Bird Alert is reached by calling 210-969-2731. The parrots move every so often, but are generally located year round in the neighborhoods of Weslaco, McAllen, Harlingen and Brownsville. Visitors can ask around or at the local chambers for specific locations. A permanent group that's popular with tourists lives at the Texas State Bank in Harlingen at 521 N. 77 Sunshine Strip. Brochures on birding in South Texas are available from the Rio Grande Valley Bird Observatory, Post Office Box 8125, Weslaco,

Parrots are now a common sight in Valley neighborhoods.

Texas, 78599.

Other great birding spots in the valley include the **Bentsen-Rio Grande Valley State Park** in Mission, the **Santa Ana National Wildlife Refuge** in Alamo and the **Sabal Palm Grove**, a National Audubon Sanctuary in Brownsville. The Rio Grande Valley is one of the top birding destinations in the United States and thousands of visitors come every year to see birds that are only found in this area. The **Rio Grande Valley Birding Festival** is held in Harlingen every year in November. The five day event includes field trips, seminars, workshops, a nature fair and art show.

"Seems the Valley is covered with wild parrots and parakeets"

★ BOB'S BEST BETS ★

All of Texas has a unique history, but in the Rio Grande Valley that history is even more unusual than most. Partly because of its climate, partly because of the close proximity to Mexico, the Rio Grande Valley has a past all its own. That past can be examined at the **Hidalgo County Historical Museum** in Edinburg.

This place has been called a "museum's museum." Its exhibits are important and well done, and they have a philosophy here that "history just is," that what's important is not the judgments you can make about the past, but the knowledge you can gain from it. In fact, a large portion of our history began in South Texas, as early as 1519 when explorers probed the river. The rapid colonization of the New World took place in New England, but the early realization of its worth happened here.

The Hidalgo County Historical Museum is an excellent interpretation of the Hispanic-accented area's colorful history and includes pioneer ranch and home items, clothing, early documents and photos. It is housed in an old jail complete with hanging tower where one convicted murderer was executed prior to the state taking over capital punishment. It was never used again. The museum is open Tuesday through Friday 9 - 5, Saturday 10 -5, Sunday 1 - 5. It is located at 121 E. McIntyre Street. Admission fee. 210-383-6911

Faith in Falfurrias

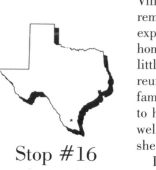

They say some memories never fade. For Delores Villarreal, it's the childhood family get-togethers she remembers most - the fiestas with their colorful pinatas exploding with candy, the smell of her mother's homemade tortillas warming on the stove. But that little girl is a grandmother herself now, and family reunions are a far more solemn occasion. In a tiny family cemetery in South Texas, she pays her respects to her mother and father, her brothers and sister - as well as a mysterious figure in a grave all alone, a man she's never even met.

Delores isn't alone in her respect for Don Pedrito Jaramillo, a shepherd from Guadalajara, Mexico. As the story goes, while herding his flock one day, he rode

A statue of Don Pedrito

into a low lying limb and was badly hurt. It is said that Don Pedrito coated his wounds with mud and was miraculously healed. It was then that Don Pedrito claimed to have had a vision in which he was told to heal others as he had healed himself.

The legacy of Don Pedrito lives on in Falfurrias today. Believers still flock every day to a shrine built around his grave. For the folks who believe in him, Don Pedrito is not a saint and certainly not a god. He is more like some friendly guardian angel still looking out for his South Texas neighbors - hand delivering their prayers and messages directly to God. People come from all over Texas and Mexico to visit the shrine and to this day it is surrounded with abandoned crutches - silent testimonials to the powers of faith. There are family photographs, business cards, even lottery tickets, each carrying the hopes and dreams of generations of believers.

If you would like to visit the Don Pedrito Shrine, take Highway 281 from Falfurrias and turn east on FM 201 to FM 1418. The shrine is on the left side of the road and is always open all day and all night. There is a curio shop where you can buy a fascinating variety of spiritual candles, herbs and mementos, which is open 9 - 5 every day. Admission is free and donations are appreciated. 512-325-2224

"Believers still flock every day to a shrine built around his grave"

★ BOB'S BEST BETS ★

They have a neat little museum in Falfurrias (the name means "the land of heart's delight") called **The Heritage Museum**. More than a hundred years ago the Texas Rangers were a shield between the pioneer settlers and the hazards of the frontier. Company D of the Rangers was stationed in Falfurrias and the museum is dedicated to the preservation of frontier heritage such as artifacts, guns, relics, records, pictures and personal papers of the Texas Rangers who were stationed here. The Heritage Museum is located at 415 N. St. Mary in Falfurrias. 512-325-2907. It's open Tuesday through Friday from 10 - 4, Saturday from 10 - 2. Admission is free. Donations are appreciated.

If you want to experience the South Texas way of life in a fun atmosphere, try the **Fiesta Ranchera**. The festival features a trailride and three kinds of music which help define the culture of this region: mariachi, country and western and conjunto music. The event is free of charge and is usually held during the first weekend of May. For more information call 512-325-3333.

Livestock, Legends and Lolo

Stop #17
Kingsville, Texas

"Lolo is a legend, and every King Ranch visitor lives his life vicariously for just a few minutes"

There are some things so Texan that we Texans almost don't believe them. We grow up with the majesty... and the myth... of this larger than life state and, after a while, the lines between legend and reality become blurred. The King Ranch is one of those places that does that to you. You hear stories about it from the time you're born. You picture one of those Western movie sets with real cowboys driving cattle for as far as you can see. Then one day you see it. Know what? It's exactly like you pictured it.

For the better part of six decades one man rode, repaired fences and rounded up millions of King Ranch livestock. Rare was the day that Alberto Villa Trevino ever ventured beyond the barbed wire boundaries of one of the world's largest ranches. The man they call "Lolo" was a cowboy's cowboy. He was raised on the ranch, always worked on the ranch and says he'll die on the ranch. He has spent more years in the saddle than any other King Ranch cowboy.

The best part for you is that Lolo is a little up in years to spend all day in a saddle. He'd still like to be roundin' up little dogies, but it's a matter of practicality. So, he does the next best thing. He spends his days telling people about it. See, these days, Lolo builds a morning fire for coffee instead of branding irons. An old Ford gets him to work instead of a trusted horse. Today, Lolo keeps his eyes peeled not for cattle in the brush, but for the next tour bus. If you're lucky, you'll be on it.

Lolo's unmatched career as a fourth generation King Ranch cowboy has elevated him to legendary status in South Texas. And it's provided him with a job that he likes just fine - telling tourists all about riding the parched pastures, rounding up strays and driving herds across the open range. Lolo meets and greets each busload of tourists, offers them some of his fresh coffee, maybe some campfire tortillas, and tells his stories. He calls his horse from a nearby corral and even demonstrates how man and mount work together to get the job done. The visitors are amazed, even the

58

Lolo, the King Ranch Legend

ones from Texas where this stuff is supposed to be common fare. Lolo is a legend, and every King Ranch visitor lives his life vicariously for just a few minutes.

The King Ranch is the largest ranch in the continental United States. These days the ranch's holdings comprise some 825,000 acres spreading over Nueces, Kenedy, Kleberg, Jim Wells, Brooks, and Willacy Counties. It is still controlled by descendants of the King and Kleberg families (Robert Kleberg married King Ranch founder Captain Richard King's youngest daughter) and the famous Running W brand is known worldwide. The Santa Gertrudis breed, the first strain of cattle originated in the Western Hemisphere, was developed on the King Ranch. Tours daily. The entrance is immediately west of Kingsville off Texas 141 and there is an admission fee. Call 512-592-8055 for guided tour times and fees. The King Ranch Visitors Center is open Monday through Saturday 9 - 4, Sunday 12 - 5. Free admission.

★ BOB'S BEST BETS ★

The city of Kingsville is located in the midst of the King Ranch, so naturally a lot of the town revolves around the ranch. The **King Ranch Museum** is located in a restored downtown ice plant and features some excellent ranch photos by the award winning photographer Toni Frissell. There is also a collection of antique coaches, vintage cars, saddles and other historic ranch items. The museum is open Monday through Saturday 10 -4, Sunday 1 - 5. Admission fee. 512-595-1881

Unsuccessful in purchasing quality saddles and leather goods in the marketplace, Captain King began operating his own saddle shop more than 120 years ago for use by his cowboys. Through the years, the **King Ranch Saddle Shop** has provided saddles and leather goods to governors, presidents and foreign heads of state. Today the shop offers a variety of leather goods and practical clothing. It is located in the historic Raglands Building downtown at 210 E. Kleberg and is open Monday through Saturday 10 - 6. 800-282-KING. By the way, you will probably run into a man on the street outside the saddle shop who will want to shine your shoes and sing you a song. Let him. He's been around for years and offers great entertainment for the price of a shine and a tip.

The **John E. Conner Museum of South Texas History** has interesting displays of Indian, Spanish, Mexican and pioneer Texas cultures. The **Kleberg Hall of Natural History** in the Conner Museum features plants and animals of South Texas in natural habitats. It is open Monday through Saturday 9 - 5 and is located on Santa Gertrudis Street on the campus of Texas A&M University-Kingsville. Free admission. 512-593-2819

The **Kingsville Visitors Center** is located at U.S. 77 and Corral Street. Open Monday through Saturday 9 - 5, Sundays 10 - 3. 800-333-5032

The Concrete Gorilla

Through the ages the world has cherished the artistry and the inspiration behind the works of the old master sculptors who chiseled the soft faces of ageless beauty and innocence. Each work of art took months, even years to produce. We in the 20th century have come to respect and admire such works. What then is the American contribution to the world's great collections of fine sculpture? It just could be the concrete gorilla.

Several years ago, David Reyckert traveled abroad and stood in awe at the great statues and sculpted works of Greece. So he came home and copied them the good old American way - in concrete! He admits it's not creative, just different. And thanks to that, the world now has "Flute Frog," "Fiddle Frog" and of course, "Guitar Dog." And don't forget "Goofy Frog," "Rose Gator," "Piglet," "Lying Pig" and "Sitting Pig." Then there's "Mr. and Mrs. Pig." The world even has "Bashful Betty" and thousands of other statues in concrete all designed not to marvel art critics, but to make your home the envy of the neighborhood.

David created so much concrete sculpture that his wife Donna was afraid friends would never be able to find their house located behind the concrete jungle. But, and trust me here, there could never be any mistaking the Reyckert's house for any other. That's because all one needs to know when searching for the Reyckerts is one tiny but very descriptive phrase - "Look for the concrete gorilla."

"Concrete Gorilla" stands guard over this classic sculpture garden like a never-moving sentry, daring anyone who would venture in with ill intentions to make it out alive. Actually, the only thing that will harm you here is if you try to move the concrete gorilla. He and the concrete rhino and concrete hippo have to be moved with heavy equipment and a big truck. They are the largest concrete statues in the world and they have become the objects of serious collectors. Not many serious collectors, but serious collectors just the same. And you, too, can be among them.

Stop #18
Odem, Texas

"They are the largest concrete statues in the world"

The boss at the Double D is a real "hard head."

Double D Statuary is located on Highway 77 between Sinton and Odem. They're open Monday through Saturday 9 - 6, Sundays 10 - 5:30. 800-418-2115. And for those in North Texas who must have a concrete gorilla of their own, or a concrete hippo or fiddling frog or such, there is now a second location on 1-35 south of Waco in Eddy. 254-859-3167

★ BOB'S BEST BETS ★

Just up I-37 is the town of George West. You'll find more liars here than any other place in Texas, but only during the **George West Storyfest**, of course! It's the biggest convention of braggarts, gossips and liars in the state. Every year on the first Saturday of November the call is sounded for anyone with a story to tell, true or not, to convene in George West. They are preserving our country's art of storytelling - the oral tradition of passing folk tales, ghost stories, legends, family history and some downright lies from one generation to the next. There are professional storytellers, locals with a good lie, cowboy poets and lots of fun and entertainment. Free admission. 512-449-2481

The Ghost of the Lexington

She was a workhorse of the war effort that sailed the high seas half a world away in defense of America. For 39 years the USS Lexington was a maritime war machine. An icon for freedom. A floating city slinging planes and pilots into battle and setting a pace that heightened the frenzied cadence of combat. But the battles fought in foreign waters have now retreated into the quiet, hidden past. They are alive today only within the aging minds and shadowed memories of the men who served aboard her.

Today the USS Lexington sits stoically in the gentle surf of the Texas coast. She is a museum now, open to all who want or need to understand why and how a country goes to war. Men like David Deal were stationed on the Lex. David's tour of duty was back in 1959. Today he is a volunteer telling tourists about life, death and what it's like to fight a war at sea. David can tell you about the time the Lex took a torpedo hit, how a kamikaze fighter plane crashed on deck, scattering torn steel and casualties from bow to stern. He will explain why the Japanese reported the Lexington sunk at least twice. What he probably can't explain is the belief by some that there are more than memories haunting the decks of the Lexington.

It seems there is a ghost aboard the USS Lexington. A sailor they say, maybe more than one. At first it seemed foolish, but then David, a decorated sailor and level-headed veteran, began to wonder. People would tour the lower levels of the Lex and return to ask David about the sailor lurking below. The young seaman didn't say anything, nothing at all. One second he was there, gone the next. When one person asked about the sailor, David dismissed it as confusion. After a second inquiry, he thought it coincidence. When several people asked, again and again, David started wondering what was going on. What was going on was dozens of reports of the same strange seaman. And it wasn't long before David had an experience that made him a believer, too. No real sighting, just strange things

Stop #19
Corpus Christi, Texas

"The young seaman didn't say anything... one second he was there, gone the next"

Some say the "Blue Ghost" really lives up to her name.

like heavy doors closing behind him all on their own. In fact, several of the volunteers aboard the Lex will tell you there's something down there.

Imagine a city of 5,000 people. Now imagine that city abandoned, empty, dark. There are corridors and passageways on the Lexington that are closed and inaccessible, others you can walk through but you might wish you had not, not alone anyway. Ghost or no ghost, the Lexington can be a very spooky place.

Now, there is no reason to be afraid because "the ghost," if there is one, appears to be friendly, so the Lexington is still a great place to visit. It's a chance to see a U.S. aircraft carrier in calm and peaceful waters. There is more than strange tales and haunted happenings anchored in Corpus Christi. The USS Lexington is an important part of our history. The Lexington is located on Corpus Christi Beach next to the Texas State Aquarium. It is open during the summer 9 - 8, and from Labor Day to Memorial Day 9 - 5. Admission fee. 800-LADY-LEX

★ BOB'S BEST BETS ★

I think Corpus Christi is one of the most interesting and charming cities in Texas. There is a certain feeling that overtakes you immediately upon arrival, almost like you're on vacation, even when you're there on business. There is so much to see and do in Corpus Christi that you should plan on spending several days in the area. While you're there, be sure and walk around downtown by the water and notice the **Kent Ullberg Sculptures**. These monumental pieces were created by a world famous artist who lives in Corpus Christi. The marina area has that "San Francisco" feel with hundreds of pleasure craft moored at neat, modern docks and slips. There are fishing boats and excursion boats based here as well as water sports equipment rentals during season. Go on Wednesday evenings and watch the sailboat races. It is scenes like this that amuse me when I talk to people who didn't know Texas had a coast!

The **Texas State Aquarium** is a place where you can experience undersea adventure and close-up views of the wonders of the water. The visit begins with an entrance through a tunnel of cascading water. It would have been easier to create this aquarium by stocking it with fish from around the world, but the founders of this place did the right thing - they stuck strictly to native sealife, only the creatures which are found in the Gulf of Mexico. Here you will see a wide variety of marine habitats - an artificial reef community created by the massive leg of an offshore oil rig, the color and beauty of the Flower Gardens Coral Reef, and a 132,000 gallon offshore exhibit where visitors can talk to a diver. In all, there are more than 125 species of the Gulf's most interesting creatures. The Conservation Pavilion is home to the endangered Kemp's Ridley Turtles and Texas River Otters. Open Monday through Saturday 9 - 6 , Sundays 10 - 6, Memorial Day through Labor Day. The rest of the year the hours are 9 - 5 Monday through Saturday and 10 - 5 on Sundays. Admission fee. 800-477-GULF

If you're the active type, you may want to consider exploring the Texas coast at sea level via a canoe or kayak. There are several companies which provide equipment and guides for this sort of thing all along the Texas coast. **Artemis Wilderness Tours** out of Austin offers its programs at nearby Matagorda and Mustang Island. It's a good way to examine the intercoastal waterways and see some of Texas waterlife and wildlife up close and personal. 800-884-3519

You can imagine what the journey to the New World must have been like with a visit to the **Ships of Christopher Columbus**. These are exact replicas of the fleet that brought the Spanish explorer to America in 1492. At this writing, the Pinta and Santa Maria are under repair, but still open to the public at a shipyard facility adjacent to the Santa Maria Plaza. Long term plans for the ships include the construction of a new dock for the Nina adjacent to the shipyard. In the meantime, visitors can learn more about "Las Carabelas" at a permanent exhibit and video theater inside the Corpus Christi Museum of Science and History. It's at 1900 N. Chaparral, open Monday - Saturday 10 - 6, Sunday 12 - 5. Admission fee. 512-883-2862

Nearby, you'll find the **Water Garden** in the **Bayfront Arts and Science Park**. Some 150 fountains are situated on steps and walls encircling visitors in a pool of relaxing sights and sounds. Shaded benches offer a break from the coastal heat. The Water Garden is just outside the **Art Museum of South Texas** at 1902 N. Shoreline Blvd. 512-884-3844

With a decidedly Mexican flavor, Corpus Christi is the last place you might expect to find it, but the **Asian Cultures Museum and Educational Center** is right on the bayfront. The attractions include the country's largest collection of hand-crafted Hakata dolls. It's at 1800 N. Mesquite and open Tuesday - Saturday, Noon - 6. Free admission, but donations are welcome. 512-993-3963

For more information on Corpus Christi, call 800-678-OCEAN.

A Way of Life Preserved in Pearland

When I was a little kid I didn't have much taste for store bought vegetables. Now most kids don't have much taste for any vegetables, but I was raised on fresh tomatoes, okra, corn and black-eyed peas in the summer months, and in the winter we ate what had been left over and canned. We grew these fresh foods in our backyard, and what we didn't grow came from Aunt Lena's farm. Truth is, I can't remember my mother ever buying vegetables at the store.

These days, I'm not sure if most kids know where the food they eat comes from. I'm not talking about just vegetables, but hamburgers and chicken fajitas. And I sure don't think most kids know the difference in the taste of fresh versus frozen and freeze dried. Too bad. But there is a place where they can find out the joys of just picked and freshly canned. It's called the Jamison Home Cannery.

Used to be, you'd always find Sheldon Smith down on his sister's farm. But times change and people retire and nowadays Sheldon only comes around during that special time of year — harvest time, when Frances Jamison is doing the canning. They've been planting down on the Jamison Farm since the days before President Roosevelt offered up a New Deal. Year in, year out, for as long as most folks can remember, the Jamisons kept the big corporate canneries supplied with figs. But when the supply exceeded the demand, the Jamisons had a problem, so Mrs. Jamison got busy and started peeling. And that was the start of the Jamison Home Cannery.

Mrs. Jamison started making fig preserves and they sold like hot cakes. One thing led to another and before long the Jamison's menu sounded more like supermarket inventory. In their own words...

"Well we have blackberry jelly and jams, dewberry jelly and jams, pickled beets and pickled okrie, cucumbers, kosher dill pickles, bread and butter pickles, hot and mild chow-chow, pickle relish, turnip

Stop #20
Pearland, Texas

"Mrs. Jamison started making fig preserves and they sold like hot cakes"

They wash their figs by hand at Jamison's.

relish, hot tomatoes, hot tomato relish, hot ripe tomato preserves, strawberry preserves, mahaw jelly, wild muscadine syrup, oranges, satsumas, and we have a little sugar fig that we sell and turnip greens and mustard, black-eyed peas, purple hull peas, lady peas and corn. We've got apple preserves, pear preserves, and blueberries, jelly and preserves. That's it."

The Jamison Home Cannery has never advertised. Never needed to. The fresh canned goods speak for themselves, and they do a lot of talking. The cannery is located on State Highway 518 between Pearland and Friendswood. They're open Monday through Saturday 8 - 6, Sundays 1 - 6. 281-485-1656

★ BOB'S BEST BETS ★

Travel south on 288 from Pearland and you'll hit a dead-end - unless you're driving some sort of marine vehicle. There are two wildlife refuges at this spot on the Gulf of Mexico worthy of your time: **Brazoria National Wildlife Refuge** just outside Danbury and **San Bernard National Wildlife Refuge** near Churchill. The Brazoria refuge is more than 43,000 acres on the Gulf Intracoastal Waterway. This is a nesting area for mottled ducks and the ancestral wintering grounds for snow geese. The folks in nearby Freeport conduct a Christmas bird count every year and the numbers are always among the highest in the nation. More than 300 different bird species have been identified here since the refuge began in 1966. There is a 6 mile self-guided tour and hiking trail. It is only open the first full weekend of every month and you must call before visiting. It is intermittently open on weekdays. 409-849-6062

The San Bernard National Wildlife Refuge is a place where snow and blue geese winter in a 27,437 acre refuge between Cedar Lake Creek and the San Bernard River on the Intracoastal Waterway. You will also see herons, egrets, and ibis on marsh ponds and lots of gulls and terns on the mud flats. Some of the mottled ducks from the Brazoria refuge seem to prefer this refuge, so you will see some here though not as many as you will at Brazoria. This refuge is open every day sunrise to sunset. It is not necessary to call first, but you can get more information by calling the Brazoria refuge at the number listed above.

Just east of Pearland you will find a truly out-of-this-world experience at **NASA/Space Center Houston**. As the visitor center for Johnson Space Center, this attraction offers tours and interactive displays of the U.S. manned space flight program. Kids Space Place, a hands-on display within the complex, includes a gravity simulator for moonwalking, a lunar rover and mock-up control with Space Shuttle, Apollo command module and Space Station. Space Center Houston is located at 1601 NASA Road 1. 800-972-0369

In nearby Lake Jackson, you'll find a fine example of a growing number of fishery centers throughout Texas. At **Sea Center Texas**, they've got rearing ponds, a saltwater marsh demonstration project, visitors center, and hatchery capable of producing 20 million fingerlings annually. Budding ichthyologists (that's a ten dollar word for fish lovers) will enjoy a visit to the "touch tanks," marine life wall displays, and large aquariums. Sea Center Texas is located at the intersection of Plantation and Medical Drives and is open Tuesday - Friday 9 - 4, Saturday 10 - 5, and Sunday 1 - 4. Free admission. 409-292-0100

A Cocoon of Tranquility

Stop #21

Houston, Texas

"Here you can lose yourself on the whisper thin wings of a butterfly"

Ah, Houston! Where shall we begin? You of course already know about the Astrodome, the ship channel, the maze of freeways. In fact there is so much to see and do in Houston that it would be silly for us to try to point you in the right direction. But that is exactly what we're going to do. Go south. Drive until you see a tall futuristic looking building that is full of insects. That's where you're going.

It's called the Cockrell Butterfly Center. At first glance it looks like a gleaming glass canister or maybe some sort of futuristic house design. In a way, it is both. This towering glass greenhouse is home to thousands of butterflies. Inside you will find a swirling mass of airborne color.

The Cockrell Butterfly Center is actually a part of the Houston Museum of Natural Science. It was built to give visitors an up close and personal look at some of the most beautiful and colorful insects in the world and to make people more aware of this side of nature. That kind of makes the butterflies the ambassadors of the insect world.

There are 6 butterfly enclosures like this one in the country and the Houston center is the tallest of them all. Inside you will find a 40 foot waterfall, a canopy of greenery and authentic heat and humidity reminiscent of a South American rain forest in miniature. Here you can lose yourself on the whisper thin wings of a butterfly. It's one of those places that recreates the wilds of nature in the middle of the city. Visit and you'll be glad you did.

The Cockrell Butterfly Center is located at One Hermann Circle Drive. From downtown Houston, take I-45 south to Hwy. 59 south. Exit Fannin Street and follow the signs to Hermann Park. Admission is $3.50 for adults and $2.50 for children. The regular hours are Monday through Saturday 9 - 6, Sundays 11 - 6, but they sometimes keep special hours during the summer. 713-639-4600

Nature in all her fragile beauty

★ BOB'S BEST BETS ★

While you're in the area and already in the unusual museum mode, stop by the **Museum of Health and Medical Science** at 1515 Hermann Drive. The medical community and hospitals in Houston are world famous and much of the medicine which was pioneered in Houston is represented in this museum. Admission fee. 713-521-1515

Also in the Museum District is the new **Holocaust Museum Houston**. A series of multimedia displays trace the rise of Nazism in Germany and the onslaught of the Holocaust. The museum is open at no charge seven days a week and is located at 5401 Caroline Street. 713-942-8000

There is some kind of festival or another going on just about every week in Houston, but the biggest is the **Houston International Festival**. The event's outstanding entertainment, food and markets honor

71

The always outlandish Art Car Parade.

cultures from around the world and sprawls across 20 downtown blocks. The most unusual event at this festival is the annual **Art Car Parade** which features vehicles covered with just about anything you can imagine such as the Orange Show's "Fruitmobile," a tutti-frutti 1967 Ford station wagon which started this outlandish happening back in 1986. Since then, others have been inspired to decorate cars with live grass, toys, picnic supplies, spray foam insulation, gold leaf and more. The International Festival happens in the spring, usually in April, over twenty days and two weekends. 1-800-4-HOUSTON or 713-654-8808

If you're looking for the really unusual, the **Orange Show** is it! This place is almost impossible to describe. It is the result of 26 years of construction by a Houston eccentric who we are sure had a motive in mind, yet no one knows for sure just what that motive was. It is a labyrinth of outdoor and indoor passages, colored tiles, folk antiques, just plain junk and native art embellished with odd mottoes and parables. From March to December, it is open Saturday and Sunday, 12 - 5; from Memorial Day to Labor Day, it is open Wednesday - Friday, 9 - 1, Saturday and Sunday 12 - 5. Small admission fee. 2402 Munger. 713-926-6368

Speaking of bizarre, Houston also has something else you don't find in just any city - the **American Funeral Service Museum**! Here you will find the nation's largest collection (who's counting?) of funeral service memorabilia, including two dozen vehicles such as horse drawn hearses, a funeral sleigh, a 1941 hearse/ambulance and a 1915 Packard "mourning bus" that carried the casket, pallbearers and 20 mourners at a top speed of 15 miles per hour. There are also Civil War cast iron caskets and turn-of-the-century embalming artifacts. Open Monday through Saturday 10 - 4, Sunday 12 - 4. 415 Barren Springs Drive. Admission fee. 713-876-3063 or 800-238-8861

And while your thoughts are already six feet under, dig a little deeper and you'll be in the famous **Houston Underground**. This is a 4 mile system of underground pedestrian tunnels that includes a variety of shops and restaurants and connects some 50 buildings beneath the streets of Houston. Route maps are available at visitors centers and at any of the banks you will encounter on your walk.

Houston was of course named for the Father of Texas, Sam Houston, who was an accomplished statesman and twice President of Texas, a Texas U.S. Senator, Commander in Chief of the Army of the Republic of Texas, Governor of Texas and Tennessee and the hero of the Battle of San Jacinto. To see the monument to this tallest of all tall Texans, you'll have to drive about 45 minutes north of Houston on I-45 to Huntsville. David Adickes is the creator of "Big Sam." He transformed 30 tons of concrete and steel into the bigger than life monument. While the real Sam Houston was a big man - 6 feet 6 inches - the colossal statue of Sam Houston is 67 feet high, is visible from over 6 miles away and is the highest point between Dallas and Houston! The **Sam Houston Statue Visitors Center** is open Tuesday through Saturday 10 - 5, Sunday 12 - 5. Drive north on I-45 to exit 109 (exit 112 if you're driving south toward Houston). 800-289-0389

A Step Back in Time

Stop #22

Galveston, Texas

"History comes alive on this island"

You will often see Galveston paired with Houston ("the Houston/Galveston area") but in our minds, Galveston is 50 miles south and at least 100 years back from Houston. It deserves its own trip because it truly is a unique Texas destination.

History comes alive on this island, a delicate stretch of land that floats two miles off the Texas coast. Long before Galveston's prosperous 19th century years, the island was the fishing and burial grounds for the Akokisa (once believed to be Karankawa) Indians and a secret hiding place for the infamous pirate Jean Laffite. Later it became the busiest and most vital port in Texas with thousands of vessels lining her harbor with bellies full of goods to build a nation. Thousands of immigrants entered the U.S. through Galveston making the port the "Ellis Island of the South." The tall ship Elissa first sailed into the port with a cargo of bananas in 1883.

Today all of these things from over a hundred years ago are celebrated in Galveston. The city's renaissance from the sleepy seaside resort town of a few years ago to the premier historic destination it is today is an ongoing process. At the heart of the island is the historic Strand District, a Victorian-era commercial center which was once a thriving center for commerce and banking. The first bank, post office and drug store in Texas were started in Galveston. Today the Strand is filled with quaint shops, art galleries, museums and restaurants. Just blocks away you can board and visit the tall ship Elissa which has been brought back to Galveston and restored to its beauty of more than a hundred years ago.

If you don't have time to see it all, the one thing we recommend is a simple little trip called Galveston Harbor Tours. This is a great way to see this port city from the water, the way thousands of people first saw her. You will pass by Elissa, hear about the glory years of Galveston, about the hurricane of 1900 which killed more than 6,000 people, and about the seawall they built to keep the waters from claiming the town again.

You will see the giant tankers which still visit this harbor today. You'll even see huge oil rigs which can be towed out to sea and placed in service drilling under the ocean. But most importantly, you will see the dolphins.

A playful dolphin makes a quick appearance for the camera.

There is something magical about dolphins. These sea mammals seem to understand us, certainly better than we understand them. And they have a desire to be with us. Each time the boats from Galveston Harbor Tours go out loaded with tourists anxious to see the city, the dolphins come, jumping from the water in matched pairs, playing their game of "Now you see me — Now you don't."

Galveston Harbor Tours is located at Pier 22, berthed behind Fisherman's Wharf Restaurant and west of Elissa. There is a dolphin watch tour every Saturday morning from 8:30 - 10 and reservations are a must. The harbor tours season runs from Memorial Day through Labor Day, Wednesday through Sunday from 12 - 5, the rest of the year, weather permitting, 12 - 3. Group tours of 30 or more are available year-round. 409-765-1700

★ BOB'S BEST BETS ★

Probably because of its importance to building this city, transportation seems to be a recurring theme in Galveston. Besides the tall ship Elissa we mentioned above, Galveston also houses three other transportation related museums. The first is the **Lone Star Flight**

Museum, at 2002 Terminal Drive, home of the **Texas Aviation Hall of Fame**. The museum houses the finest and largest collection of restored to flying condition vintage military aircraft in the southern United States. Open daily 10 - 5. Admission fee. 409-740-7722

The second transportation related collection is found at the **Center for Transportation and Commerce**, more commonly known as the **Galveston Island Railroad Museum**. This is one of the most interesting collections of its type anywhere. On once active tracks you will find 46 vintage railroad cars and steam engines. The historic Santa Fe Depot has been restored to 1932 art deco style and there is an HO-gauge working model of the Port of Galveston with tracks, ships and port activities. Possibly the best exhibit is the collection of life-sized figures which depicts a busy depot scene of the 1930s. Some of the figures "speak" to visitors, telling their story and the story of Galveston as they talk. Located on Rosenberg Street (25th Street) at the foot of the Strand. Call 409-765-5700 for schedule times. Free parking. Admission fee.

The third of the transportation museums is the **David Taylor Classic Car Museum**, a collection which is divided into three categories: antiques, classics and muscle cars - but no imports. This is strictly a tribute to the American automobile. 1918 Mechanic Street. Admission fee. Open daily 10 - 5. 409-765-6590

While in Galveston, be sure to visit some of the fine restored mansions such as **Ashton Villa** (2328 Broadway), **Bishop's Palace** which is Galveston's most celebrated landmark and is the state's only structure on the list of the nation's 100 outstanding buildings (1402 Broadway), and **Moody Mansion and Museum**, a prime example of Richardsonian Romanesque architecture (2618 Broadway).

For more information on Galveston, contact the Convention and Visitors Bureau at 888-GAL-ISLE.

City of Energy

Funny how one event can change everything. For Beaumont, Texas, that event occurred on January 10, 1901, when the Lucas Gusher blew in at the Spindletop salt dome just south of town. "Oil" became the biggest brag in Beaumont. An entire industry was born and huge corporations such as Texaco, Mobil and Gulf got their start - all because of the one event now known as "Spindletop."

Today Beaumont has a population of over 114,000. It is a thriving, dynamic city with a colorful past and exciting future. What may surprise you is that there are 19 museums here, giving Beaumont its nickname, "Museum Capital of Texas." And it is here that you will find a wonderful shrine to a great Texan - Thomas Alva Edison!

Okay, so old Thomas Edison wasn't really a Texan. In fact, he was what some would call the "Anti-Texan." Edison was from New Jersey. But there is a connection causing his museum to be located in Beaumont - electricity. No, he didn't invent the stuff, just showed us how to use it. And use it. And use it some more. So why an Edison museum here in Beaumont? Well, it seems Gulf States Utilities Company is in the business of making electricity, and they figure they wouldn't be in that business if not for Edison. And they happen to have a very historic electrical substation, the first building to distribute electricity in Texas. Reason enough.

When you think of Edison, chances are you think first of the electric light bulb. He experimented with 9,000 different kinds of bulbs and actually invented the word "filament." The light bulb was a great example of his genius. But he did so much more. Try to imagine the world without light, motion pictures or the phonograph. Edison gave us all of those and they give us some idea of his greatness. When Thomas Edison opened his first laboratory he set two goals: Come up with a major invention every six weeks and a minor one every ten days. He did both and the numbers add up to one invention every other week of Edison's life!

Stop #23
Beaumont, Texas

"They have a historic electrical substation, the first building to distribute electricity in Texas"

Edison had 1093 patents, the first being for the Electric Vote Counter which he invented for the United States Congress. He couldn't sell it because they didn't want their votes recorded, so Edison vowed all his other inventions would be things people needed or wanted. Among the things Edison thought we wanted and needed are the electric toaster, the first electric razor, the perfection of telegraph equipment, the talking doll, the Dictaphone, the electric car battery, a submarine detector and all kinds of sockets, fuses and generators. You can also hear him speak the first words ever recorded, "Mary had a little lamb." You can even see Edison's "violet ray machine" which he touted as a cure for baldness and ingrown toenails.

Edison finds a home in Texas.

The Edison Museum is located in the old Travis Street substation which is still a part of Beaumont's electrical system. From Interstate 10 take the downtown exit and turn left on Calder which will become Main Street. Turn left on Mulberry which will end in front of the Edison Museum at 350 Pine. Open Monday through Friday 1 - 3:30, but for other times call 409-981-3089. Free admission.

★ BOB'S BEST BETS ★

Ever wonder where firefighters learn to be firefighters? One place is right here in Beaumont at the **Fire/Rescue Training Center**. The local Beaumont area fire departments train here in hazardous materials, rescue and fire fighting, and it is also home of the Lamar University Fire and Hazardous Materials Training Program which is one of only four OSHA approved training schools in the nation. Public tours are welcome. 409-839-4307

You'll also want to visit the **Fire Museum of Texas**, a 1927 former fire station where you will see displays of antique fire bells, leather buckets, nozzles, badges and vintage fire engines. Housed in the old central fire station at 400 Walnut. Free admission. Open Monday through Friday, 8 - 4:30. 409-880-3927

Spindletop and the boomtown that grew around it are recreated in modern-day Beaumont with the **Spindletop/Gladys City Boomtown Museum**. It's on US 69 South at University Drive. Open Tuesday through Sunday, 1 - 5. Admission fee. 409-835-0823

Not far from Beaumont is Port Arthur, hometown of about as wide a variety of celebrities as you'll ever come across — from football coach Jimmy Johnson to 60s rock icon Janis Joplin. You may remember Janis wailing, "Lord, won't you buy me a Mercedes-Benz," but this loud lady actually drove a psychedelic-colored Porsche, which can be found today in the **Southeast Texas/Southwest Louisiana Musical Heritage Room** of the **Museum of the Gulf Coast**. Along with memorabilia from the "Big Bopper" J.P. Richardson, Jr., Richie Valens, and Tex Ritter, you'll discover historical artifacts throughout the museum. It's at 701 Fourth Street. Open Monday through Saturday, 9 - 5; Sunday, 1 - 5. Admission fee. 409-982-7000

Port Arthur celebrates Joplin's birthday with an annual festival held during the second week of January. The **Janis Joplin Birthday Bash** features the music of Southeast Texas including Cajun, rhythm & blues, and country. 409-985-7822

Play a Pine in Groveton

Stop #24
Groveton, Texas

"Finally, Maria feels she is once again in the company of ancient voices"

Few people in the world can say they've heard the true voice of a tree. Maria Minnaar has done just that among the pines of East Texas. She has found a singing voice that strikes a note deep down in her soul. For years she has listened to this voice that comes from the woods.

Maria was the child of a missionary and was raised in the most remote parts of Africa. There she learned to make and play a musical instrument called a marimba. Its sound is as much a part of the sound of Africa as ancient tribal drums. For centuries the marimba was crafted from a rare African wood which is now in short supply. After coming to Texas and experimenting with the native trees, Maria discovered she could closely reproduce the unique sound of the marimba by playing on pine... good, old, common as ants East Texas yellow pine. In fact, it provides a tonal quality that she says rivals the finest African marimba ever made. Finally, Maria feels she is once again in the company of ancient voices. The voice of the marimba. Other folks hear the voices, too, and have followed the sound all the way to Maria's front door.

Outdoor acoustics are better than any concert hall.

Maria doesn't just make marimbas. She's teaching the locals in Groveton how to play the ancient musical instrument. Now Groveton High School has what is probably the only football game half-time marimba band in the world. Without flutes or fiddles, these musicians have developed quite a following with concert dates filling up fast and a CD out in the stores!

Maria searched all over the world before landing in East Texas to play and make marimbas. Now you can hear it, too. You can even buy one if you like. Just drop by Maria's workshop near Groveton. If you're lucky, you might catch Maria assembling a handmade marimba, or even a rehearsal by Maria's students. Please call ahead before visiting. 409-642-2714

★ BOB'S BEST BETS ★

Groveton sits at the southeast entrance to the **Davy Crockett National Forest**, one of the most beautiful spots in Texas. Its 161,000 acres contain canoe trails, hiking trails and lakes. If you like great scenery and getting out in nature, try the **Kickapoo Recreation Area**, about one-and-a-half miles southeast of Groveton on U.S. 287 and **Big Slough Canoe Trail and Wilderness Area** on the Neches River near Neches Bluff. Also in the area are the **Angelina National Forest, Sabine National Forest** and **Sam Houston National Forest**. 409-639-8501

The lumber industry in East Texas has provided building materials and jobs for decades. In Lufkin, you'll want to drop by the **Texas Forestry Museum** at 1905 Atkinson Drive, where you'll find leaf and tree identifications, early logging machinery, antique railroad and sawmill steam engines and such. Open Monday through Saturday, 10 - 5; Sunday 1 - 5. Admission is free, but donations are appreciated. 409-632-9535

Just north of Lufkin is Nacogdoches, the site of an Indian settlement for centuries before the first Europeans arrived. Here you will want to see **El Camino Real**, "The King's Highway," which is thought to be the first major thoroughfare in the state, and **La Calle del Norte**, currently North Street in Nacogdoches, believed to be the oldest public thoroughfare in the United States. For more information on Nacogdoches, call 409-564-7351.

The Birth of the Peanut Pattie

Stop #25

Jacksonville, Texas

There's a joke in my family... one of those you hear your whole life, that you always know is coming... that has to do with dessert. It goes something like this: We're eating in a restaurant and the waitress says, "Did y'all save room for dessert?" My dad will always say, "I'll have a peanut pattie." Har, har, har. The nicer the restaurant, the better the joke. Problem is, my dad's really not joking. He wants a peanut pattie.

I was raised on those things. A Dr Pepper and Peanut Pattie was always one step above an RC and a Moon Pie. It was tradition in our house. And we owe it all to W. L. Holcomb in Jacksonville, Texas. On October 22, 1924, W. L. Holcomb decided to start his own candy company. One of the first things he noticed when he started his company was that peanuts were easy to come by and didn't cost nearly as much as pecans and walnuts. So W. L. Holcomb came up with a peanut product, something he called the peanut pattie,

Packin' peanut patties for nigh on 75 years

and delivered them in his Model T Roadster. He soon discovered that the peanut pattie was especially popular with the workers who labored in the lumber mills and at remote job sites. They could just unwrap one and eat it easily right there, so W. L. sold a bunch of peanut patties.

Today Holcomb Candy Company (also known as Jacksonville Candy Company) makes all kinds of candy. W. L. Holcomb worked until he was in his upper 90s, then decided it was time to retire, but the company is still run by the Holcomb family and they still make peanut patties. They also make peanut brittle, "peco" bars, peanut logs and coconut bars.

Holcomb Candy Company is located at 218 Woodrow Street in Jacksonville. There is a factory store open Monday through Friday 8 - 4, where you can purchase their patties and other products, but this isn't the only place you can find them. Seems a gentleman from Arkansas had a passion for their patties and put them in his stores around the country. Before he died a few years ago, Sam Walton was said to have still preferred peanut patties over most other desserts. Tours are offered September through Christmas. Call 903-586-8334 for times.

"A Dr Pepper and Peanut Pattie was always one step above an RC and a Moon Pie"

★ BOB'S BEST BETS ★

Jacksonville seems to be the place for unique companies. One of them is Jacksonville's **Texas Basket Company**. If you've ever picked a peck of practically anything, chances are you've hauled it home in a Jacksonville basket. It's one of the only basket companies left in the nation. Martin Swanson operates the basket company. He makes his product from East Texas Sweetgum which is sawed, boiled, bent and branded in this more than 80-year-old factory. These days people buy the baskets more for decorations. Hwy. 79 at Myrtle Drive. Self-guided tours are available Monday through Friday, 8 - 4. Guided tours for 12 or more can be arranged by calling 903-586-8014. The factory store is open Monday through Saturday, 8 - 5. Additional hours October through December include Sunday, 1 - 5.

Mrs. Lee's Garden

Stop #26

Gladewater, Texas

Remember the popular television program of the 70s called "The Waltons?" There were some Waltons made-for-TV movies, too, and my favorite I think was called "The Homecoming." Anyway, the point is, Daddy Walton didn't make it home for Christmas and everyone was worried and disappointed and at the last minute he shows up with a story about running into Santa Claus to explain how he happened to have gifts for everyone. John Boy got a writing tablet and Mary Ellen got something else and on and on, and then he came to Mama Walton. He brought her flowers. Just flowers. A pretty bouquet of some sort and she was thrilled, absolutely thrilled. And then she muttered a line that, for some reason, stuck with me. She said, "Flowers. In the dead of winter."

In Gladewater daffodils bloom despite the cold.

That's how I felt when I ran across Mrs. Lee's Garden outside Gladewater. It was February and there was a little snow on the ground (pretty unusual for Texas) and suddenly there were thousands and thousands of daffodils! They were everywhere, as far as you could see, scattered throughout the forest in all their golden glory. And I remember I actually said it...out loud, with no one else around to hear me. Flowers. In the dead of winter.

Helen Lee was a wonderful woman who loved nature and loved people. She wanted the two to enjoy each other, so she planted thousands of daffodils on her land, then provided in her will that this incredible place would live on long after she was gone. She named it Daffodil Dale, but the official name is the Helen Lee Estate Daffodil Gardens. There are more than 50 acres of daffodils and you can visit them for yourself. Mrs. Lee would be glad to have you.

From Loop 285, take U.S. 271 south about 5 miles, then a mile east on County Road 3103. Open mid-February through early March, but call ahead because sometimes they have to close due to road conditions or weather. Admission is free. 903-845-5780

"Flowers... in the dead of winter"

★ BOB'S BEST BETS ★

Just about every town has some kind of nickname. Gladewater is known as the **"Antique Capital of East Texas."** I wonder why they didn't just claim the whole state. There are more than two dozen antique and craft shops, enough to keep you busy all day or more. If that's not enough, you can visit during the **Arts and Crafts Festival**. It's usually held in late September outdoors at the Broadway School and offers about 320 booths and vendors. Call the Gladewater Chamber of Commerce for more information. 800-627-0315

If you're lucky, while you're visiting Gladewater you'll catch a performance of the **Silly Symphony**. This is one of those senior citizens bands where the members play just about everything available.

There's so much to do in Gladewater, you might not be able to squeeze it all into one day, so take your time and spend the night in the local "B & B," Bed and... Bakery! That's right, **Glory Bee Honeycomb Suites** offers romantic accommodations conveniently located atop a full-size bakery/restaurant. Dieters beware though — the scent of Susan Morgan's homemade brownies wafting upstairs can be absolute torture! Glory Bee is at 111 N. Main Street. 800-594-2253

Music Box Mania

Stop #27

Sulphur Springs, Texas

Funny how you sometimes find the strangest things in the strangest places. Sulphur Springs is a good example. Over the years of traveling the backroads I've spent quite a bit of time in Sulphur Springs. In the early days of producing our television show this town was a place we visited time and again. There were always lots of good stories in Sulphur Springs and lots of good characters. Men like Leo St. Clair.

I met Leo sometime in the early 1970s when I was standing on the square in Sulphur Springs looking at their monumental courthouse and a man told me to "go see what's in the library." That man, as it turned out, was the originator and collector of what was in the library - a collection of incredible music boxes. Mr. St. Clair explained that he always loved music boxes and started his collection when the Belgian royal family gave him a music box as a gift. After that, he said everyone gave him music boxes. "Suddenly it became very easy to shop for me," he told me. "My collection grew and grew."

Leo's music boxes come in all shapes and sizes.

Leo arranged for his incredible music box collection to be on display in the Sulphur Springs library. After his death, the mini-museum became the property and pride of Sulphur Springs. Today there are more than 150 music boxes on display. Music Box Gallery is located at 201 North Davis. Open Monday through Friday, 9 - 6. Note: As of this writing, there are plans for a new library in Sulphur Springs and the music box collection will be moved at that time. It's best to call ahead. Admission is free, but donations are appreciated. 903-885-4926

★ BOB'S BEST BETS ★

At last count (and they count fairly often) Hopkins County was not only the leading dairy county in Texas, but in the entire United States as well with at least 490 dairies! That's a lot of cow and a lot of milk. Milk, by the way, is a real pride and joy around these parts because Wisconsin boasts lots of dairies and dairy cows but most of their milk goes into the production of cheese. "Ours," folks in Hopkins County boast, "is good enough to drink!"

To find out the complete story of the dairy industry, visit the **Southwest Dairy Center**. It looks like a big old dairy barn, complete with its own silo. Inside you can hear the story of how milk was produced in the good old days. You can even see an early day barn scene and a kitchen scene where mom separates the milk from the cream and the kids churn butter. There's an old time soda fountain where you can get a pretty good chocolate malted or milk shake and a gift shop with some unique "cow gifts" for sale. The Dairy Center even has a mobile dairy classroom in which a cow and calf are taken to area schools to teach kids who think milk is made in the grocery store where it really originates! The Southwest Dairy Center is in the Civic Center Complex at 1210 Houston Street. Open Monday through Saturday, 9 - 4. Admission is free, but donations are appreciated. 903-439-6455

"Mr. St. Clair started his collection when the Belgian royal family gave him a music box as a gift"

Cowboy Jesus

Traveling the backroads you run into lots of mysteries. Some have easy answers. Others remain elusive and continue to make you wonder. The Evergreen Cemetery in Paris, Texas, makes you wonder.

No, this isn't that old joke about why they buried all those people there. (I hope no punch line is necessary.) Fact is, Evergreen Cemetery is an interesting place for three reasons:

1. It's huge. There are more than 50,000 people buried there and the graves date back to 1866. Some of the people laid to rest at Evergreen Cemetery were early Texas patriots.

Stop #28

Paris, Texas

"This Jesus is wearing cowboy boots"

Those are boots peekin' out from underneath the robe.

2. The headstones. With so many graves, I guess some of the people buried there wanted theirs to, well, stand out. They must have wanted them to look different, so there are lots of very unusual markers and monuments at Evergreen Cemetery.

3. Cowboy Jesus. That's our name for this very strange marker, and it's the real reason we want you to visit. This is a mystery we've wondered about for the past 15 or 20 years at least. And still no answer. See, right there in the midst of the Evergreen Cemetery, with all those graves and all those unusual markers, is a statue of Jesus. That in itself is not at all unusual. But look toward the ground, beneath the long robe. This Jesus is wearing cowboy boots! And no one, to our knowledge, knows why. It's called the Babcock Monument and it stands 12 feet tall. Go see for yourself. And let us know if you find out the answer.

The Evergreen Cemetery at 560 Evergreen is open sunrise to sunset 7 days a week. Look for Willet Babcock's grave with the large statue of Jesus. We'd tell you where to look, but half the fun is finding it!

★ BOB'S BEST BETS ★

I really like it when I find unusual and top quality things in smaller towns. The **Hayden Museum of American Art** is one of those places the big cities would like to have. There are four galleries and the biggest one has a permanent collection of graphic art, archival photography and American chairs! There is an outstanding art library and admission is free, but it is suggested you call ahead and make an appointment. 930 Cardinal Lane. 903-785-1925

The second largest **Eiffel Tower** in the second largest Paris in the world is also found in this town. Right there on the corner of Jefferson Road and South Collegiate Drive is a replica of the Eiffel Tower in Paris, France. This Texas version is about 65 feet tall and was built by the Boiler Makers Union Local #902 using donated materials. For more information on Paris, call the Chamber of Commerce at 903-784-2501.

The Singing Drywall Man

Stop #29
Greenville, Texas

Some of the best places to visit are naturally going to be the hardest to pin down. Some of these suggestions we're making are more than just a matter of dropping by. They require timing. If you want to see the singing drywall man, you'll have to time it right.

Big Bill Johnson makes his living building walls. Actually, he covers and textures the walls after they've been "framed." He puts up sheetrock, tapes and beds it and slaps some "mud" on it. Big Bill's been making his living this way for a long time.

But there's another side to Big Bill Johnson. He's an entertainer, a performing musician and songwriter. Lots of folks say they do these things, but our buddy Big Bill has worked with and for some of the best — stars like Willie Nelson and some other big country names. No, Bill is no headliner on the Grand Ole Opry and he doesn't have a string of country hits like George Strait. Still, the Willies and Georges of country music know and love Big Bill Johnson. So do we.

You can catch Big Bill Johnson "jamming" with his buddies and playing his music at the Pickle Brothers'

Big Bill's music is pure country.

Lumberyard in Greenville. If Big Bill had it his way, he'd be there on a regular basis at least once a week, but he has to make a living slingin' mud on walls, so sometimes he doesn't make it. Like I said, you'll have to time it right to get to hear him. If you do, you'll likely go away loving life just a little bit more and won't be able to get one of Big Bill's original tunes out of your head. Songs like the one about himself:

> I'm a drywall man (I'm a drywall man!)
> I'm a drywall man (I'm a drywall man!)
> I got mud in my blood
> I'm a drywall man!

To find out Big Bill Johnson's schedule call ahead. 903-454-2255

"You can catch Big Bill "jamming" with his buddies at the Pickle Bros. Lumberyard"

★ BOB'S BEST BETS ★

Paul Mathews Prairie Nature Preserve is a 100 acre native prairie meadow just west of Greenville that's never been plowed. It is part of the once vast (12 million acre) Texas Blackland Prairie and today is one of the few remaining untouched pieces of ground where you can see the land the way our forefathers saw it. Meadowlarks and red-winged blackbirds feed on the grass and birders will think this area is a paradise, not just on Mathews Prairie but at nearby Tawakoni and Cooper Lakes where bald eagles, kestrels, and red-tailed hawks can be easily spotted. To visit Mathews Prairie go west from Greenville on U.S. 380 about 4 and a half miles and follow the signs.

At one time, Greenville was well known as the Cotton Capital of the World, and in 1912 the Greenville Cotton Compress set the world's record for the number of bales pressed in a day and loaded into freight cars. You can see the history of the crop that is the heritage of Greenville at the **American Cotton Museum** where they actually grow and pick a crop every year as part of the museum's demonstration program. Open Tuesday through Saturday, 10 - 5. Admission fee. 600 I-30 East. 903-450-4502

The Chautauqua Revival

There was a time, long before the glass and steel skyscrapers, when native Americans camped on the banks of Browder Springs. Back in the early days of John Neely Bryan's village on the Trinity, this was a gathering place where families spent lazy summer afternoons in the city's first public park. But that was then, and this is now, and today Dallas' Old City Park is moving forward... to its past.

Back in the late 19th century, before everyone had a car or a phone, much less internet and cable television, isolation was a way of life. A trip to your nearest neighbor could be an all day affair, and news from some areas of the country could be months in coming. Then a new trend swept across the nation and changed all that. Performers and lecturers came to town and a new way of life arrived with them. This just may have been the earliest beginnings of our shrinking world. It was called the Chautauqua Movement. Teddy Roosevelt called it "the most American thing in America."

Chautauqua, essentially, was an adult education movement aimed at exposing people outside of the Eastern seaboard towns to America's culture. Shakespearean plays, music, jugglers and yodelers would arrive and perform. Poets would recite. Lecturers would read and discuss. It all took place inside something called a Chautauqua pavilion, and at one time there were lots of them spread across the United States. Mass use of telephones, then radio and finally television, coupled with America's preoccupation with the family automobile and U.S. highways, quickly made Chautauqua unnecessary. The movement disappeared almost as soon as it arrived.

Today, there is only one authentic Chautauqua pavilion remaining in Texas, and that one is in Waxahachie, 30 miles south of Dallas. But since Dallas' Old City Park is in the business of telling Texans about their past, they have assembled an entire 19th century town complete with homes, churches, schools, shops, and other authentic structures. The one

Stop #30

Dallas, Texas

"Performers and lecturers came to town and a new way of life arrived with them"

The Chautauqua movement is alive and well in Dallas.

thing that was missing: a Chautauqua pavilion. Since Waxahachie wasn't about to let go of theirs, the only thing to do was to build one. Today, Old City Park proudly presents its new old Chautauqua pavilion. You know what? It's just as splendid as the real thing!

Old City Park is located at 1717 Gano Street off I-30 in the shadow of the Dallas skyline. The park is open Tuesday through Saturday 10 - 4, Sundays 12 - 4. Admission fee. 214-421-5141

★ BOB'S BEST BETS ★

We have the same problem in Dallas as we had in Houston. Where do you start? There is so much to see and do here that you can easily spend weeks and only scratch the surface. But our aim is to send you to those special places that you might not find without help, those places that offer something you can't find just anywhere. In Dallas, one of those places is **White Rock Lake**.

I grew up around White Rock Lake. In fact, over the years I've lived on just about every side of it. Dallasites have a way of defining themselves by this lake. Neighborhoods are described as being on the east side of the lake or just past the spillway or just the other side of White Rock Creek. New York has its Central Park. Dallas has White Rock Lake.

Boaters set sail on White Rock Lake.

There are some incredible mansions along Lawther Drive which makes its way around the lake. Billionaire oilman H. L. Hunt's replica of Mount Vernon is here. There is a great bike and jogging path around the lake, one of the first of its kind in the country. The sailboats are wonderful to watch and the fishing's not bad either. But the thing about White Rock is its wildlife. As Dallas has grown out farther and farther into its suburbs, the critters that once inhabited this city have been chased away. Recently, though, the animals seem to have figured out that the lake's a safe place to live, and they've come back. Like urban pioneers, nearly 300 species - more than a quarter of all Texas wildlife species protected by state and federal law - now call the 2,100 acre White Rock Lake Park their home. In fact, the Dallas Park and Recreation Department has applied for and received designation for White Rock as an Urban Wildlife Sanctuary. All this smack dab in the middle of the big city!

When I was a teenager growing up in Dallas, the purpose of White Rock Lake was obviously human pleasure with kids crowding the park every weekend. Today, we humans take a back seat to the lake's wildlife. Previously manicured areas are now allowed to grow tall to give some protection to the critters. Wildflowers are allowed to take over and fallen trees sometimes just stay where they fall, providing natural shelters. The mammals, reptiles, amphibians, fish and birds have taken back their park. Even animals like bobcats and foxes, long ago thought to have vanished from this part of Texas, have been spotted at White Rock.

The best time to see the wildlife at White Rock Lake is early morning and late evening. You may not actually see the animals. In fact, it's probably best for them if you don't, but you can have a great time watching for their tracks and other signs of wildlife inhabitation. One word of caution: Please don't approach any wildlife you do see and never disturb their homes (nests, dens, etc.) Remember: This is their park now and the laws are on their side!

White Rock Lake is between Garland Road, Northwest Highway and Mockingbird Lane. There are several entrances to the park accessible from these roads. If you really have some time to kill, walk the entire distance around the lake. It's a beautiful, interesting hike and there is no telling what you'll see along the way.

Speaking of unusual sights you won't believe your eyes when you visit **Pioneer Plaza**. This four acre site between the historic Pioneer Cemetery and the Dallas Convention Center features the sculptures of 70 Texas Longhorn Steers on a cattle drive. It's the world's largest bronze monument! Between Young and Griffin Streets.

A Cattle Baron's Wedding Gift

"Get a peek into the lives of a turn of the century family that helped make Texas and Ft. Worth what they are today"

Let's get one thing straight right up front. The thing some people call *The Metroplex* exists only in the minds of television newscasters. There is no grand alliance of North Central Texas towns and there is no entity called *The Twin Cities*. Dallas and Fort Worth may be only 30 miles apart, but they are separated by a cultural line bigger than the both of them. While Dallas is modern and Oz-like, Fort Worth is Old West and very Texan - not that Fort Worth is the least bit backward or in any way less than its bigger neighbor to the east - it is not. The Convention and Visitors Bureau likes to explain it by saying, "Fort Worth is the way you want Texas to be." Fort Worth has a kind of quality of life and sophistication that makes it a very special place. And it's been that way at least since the turn of the century, when a place called Thistle Hill was built.

A newlywed cottage for two would never do - not for the daughter of one of America's greatest cattle barons. Electra Waggoner had been among cattle and cowhands all her life. After a European honeymoon, she and her new husband, A. B. Wharton, wanted a more sophisticated lifestyle. With his precious daughter's heart set on leaving Decatur, W. T. Waggoner built the couple the grandest mansion of Quality Hill, Fort Worth in 1904. They called it Rubismont. Translated it means Thistle Hill.

The architects of Thistle Hill knew how to please their Texas clients. They knew how to design and build things a little grander than they would elsewhere, things like over-sized staircases, doors and windows. As you enter Thistle Hill, your eyes will immediately go to the horseshoe-shaped staircase with the golden oak treatment and to the palladium window with two Tiffany-style stained glass windows. And in the dining room, visitors will find Haviland and Limoges china collected by the owners — all this opulent finery paid for with money earned on the rugged ranches and smelly stockyards of Texas!

Today, everything is restored to the grandeur of the original Wharton house. But just a few years ago,

After years of neglect, Thistle Hill glows with new life.

Electra Waggoner herself probably would not have recognized it. There were holes in the ceiling, rotting wood throughout and vagrants living inside. It might have met the wrecking ball if not for some concerned preservationists who raised the money to buy and restore it.

Thistle Hill is now open to the public and thousands of people visit her every year. What's more, Electra's "honeymoon cottage" now hosts up to 140 weddings and receptions annually! At Thistle Hill, visitors see an incredible home filled with precious mementos and priceless antiques, but most of all they get a peek into the lives of a turn of the century family that helped make Texas, and Fort Worth, what they are today.

Thistle Hill is open Monday through Friday 10 - 3, Sunday 1 - 4. Guided tours begin on the hour. It is located at 1509 Pennsylvania Avenue. Admission fee. 817-336-1212

★ BOB'S BEST BETS ★

When it comes to museums in Texas, Fort Worth has the best of the best with the **Kimball Art Museum**, **Amon Carter Museum** and the **Museum of Science and History**. One in particular that is not as well known is the **Sid Richardson Collection of Western Art**. This tiny place on Main Street contains the outstanding collection of the late Fort Worth oilman whose name it carries. The permanent collection of 56 paintings by Frederic Remington and Charles M. Russell reflect both the art and reality of the American West. If you happen to have a print by either of these Western Art masters, you will probably see the original here. 309 Main Street. Open Tuesday and Wednesday 10 - 5, Thursday and Friday 10 - 8, Saturday 11 - 8 and Sunday 1 - 5. Admission is free. 817-332-6554

The Sid Richardson Collection is located in an area of downtown Fort Worth known as **Sundance Square**. Fort Worth has managed to do with its downtown area what most American cities have been trying to do for two or three decades, and Sundance Square is part of the success. This award winning area features restaurants, live theaters, shopping and the acclaimed **Caravan of Dreams**, a sanctuary for the performing arts. This is one of the Southwest's few avant-garde performing arts centers, with blues and jazz bands performing regularly along with top-name recording artists.

The Cultural District is home to one of our favorite spots to unwind — the **Botanic Garden**. It's a showcase of 150,000 living plants representing 2,500 species. Don't miss the 10,000-square-feet glass conservatory. It holds 2,500 tropical plants native to both Central and South America. From April through November, the conservatory is open Monday through Friday 10 - 9, Saturday 10 - 6, Sunday 1 - 6. From November through March, the hours are the same except for closing at 4 pm on the weekends. The garden is north of I-30 on University Drive across from Trinity Park. The conservatory is located at 3220 Botanic

Garden Boulevard. Entrance to the botanic garden is free, but there's a fee for the conservatory and Japanese Garden. Admission to the grounds is free from 8 am to dusk. 817-871-7686

A touch of the Old West in downtown Fort Worth

Another area of Fort Worth you won't want to miss is the famous **Stockyards**. This National Historic District was once the center of this town's cattle business, and some buying, selling and trading of livestock still goes on here. Today though, the Fort Worth Stockyards is mostly a collection of shops, restaurants and Western theme bars reminiscent of the old frontier town days. Of particular interest are **Billy Bob's Texas**, a huge entertainment complex which claims to be the world's largest honky-tonk, and the **White Elephant Saloon**, an authentic Western tavern. If you're very lucky, famous Western singer and songwriter Don Edwards will be performing during your visit. For more information, call the Convention and Visitor's Bureau at 800-433-5747.

The Store that Time Forgot

Stop #32

Rosston, Texas

I admit I have wanderlust. I must have been born with it, because I've wanted to go, go, go as long as I can remember. I love to visit places I've never been, to meet new people and find out things I've always wondered about. I'm never satisfied staying in one place too long. And I envy people who are content doing the same things day in, day out, right there in the same place where they've always done it. People like Nick Muller.

Interstate 35 is a fast moving road that will take you all the way from Mexico to Canada. But if you get off the interstate just south of Gainesville and drive about 20 minutes west, you'll find yourself in a world you may not know still exists. You'll find yourself in Rosston. And right in the middle of Rosston, right there where you see folks gathered on the bench against that outside wall, is Nick Muller's place, the Rosston General Store.

Take a look around. They may not have everything you want here but they pretty much have everything you need. Soap and cereal, Babo and bread. But the most important things you'll find here at the Rosston General Store aren't for sale. You'll have to earn them.

The century-old centerpiece of Rosston.

They're called trust. And friendship. And conversation. Don't expect to get these things on your first visit, or even your second. They're hard to come by and pretty expensive.

The Rosston General Store has been open since 1879. These days it's run by a young man named Nick Muller. When we first met Nick he was barely voting age. Day in, day out, he was there at the store. He was there because the people of Rosston count on it. They depend on him. And he can't let them down. Even though Nick's never been anywhere. Not to speak of, anyway. "I've been to Antlers, Oklahoma," he told me. "And I've been just a little bit south of Dallas one time. Oh yeah, and I almost went to Amarillo. That's all."

Imagine that. A young man who's content doing what he's been doing right there where he's been doing it - because people depend on him. Oh, Nick's got dreams, but he's in no hurry to live them. "I think a fella oughta see the ocean sometime in his life," he said. We're sure Nick will do that someday. If he can ever get away.

Nick Muller's Rosston General Store is located on FM 922 west of Interstate 35 out of Valley View, Texas. Open Monday through Saturday, 7 - 6. Gone to church on Sunday. 940-768-2239

"The most important things you'll find here at the Rosston General Store aren't for sale"

★ BOB'S BEST BETS ★

If they, or you, are looking for a little more action, Gainesville isn't that far away. Mention Gainesville to people in any other town within a 100 mile radius of this Cooke County seat and most will immediately think of the **Gainesville Factory Outlet Shops**. If shopping is your game, you'll want to play it in Gainesville.

The town is also famous for its historic homes. There are at least 26 historic houses in Gainesville, beautiful 19th century **Victorian Homes** built along brick-paved streets. Drive down Church, Lindsay and Denton Streets and you'll see most of them.

An Old Stetson's Salvation

Stop #33
Wichita Falls, Texas

"Stanley claims she can tell a lot about you — just by your hat"

Next to a beat-up old pair of boots, there's nothing quite as personal to a cowboy as his hat. Even if it's old, roughed up and full of holes and trail dust, the hat is the cowpoke's best friend. At the Huskey's Hat Company in Wichita Falls they love dirty hats. If you've got a stained Stetson or a beat-up Bailey, Stanley Rater will see to it that it's washed, blocked, steamed, creased and restored to almost as good as new. Yep, Stanley Rater is a hatter who can renovate Resistols.

Now, don't let the name Stanley throw you. Stanley's no rough and tumble cowhand. This Stanley's a cow<u>girl</u>, and she knows her hats. Stanley used to make hats, too, but making old hats look new keeps her plenty busy these days. She says it's easy to be a hatter.

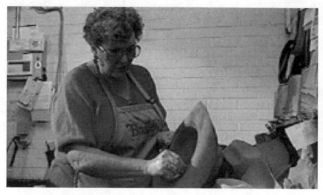

Stanley loves old hats – the dirtier the better!

All you need is a couple of decades of experience and a feel for felt. There is nothing new about hat cleaning and Stanley's antique machines are evidence of that. What's even more old-fashioned is the hands-on care your hat will get at Stanley Rater's. When she's finished, Stanley claims she can tell a lot about you - just by your hat. She will know if you're right-handed or left-handed and whether you put your hat on holding the brim or the crown. If you smoke or chew tobacco, she'll know that, too.

If you've got a dirty old hat and don't mind spending about 25-bucks, drop by the Huskey's Hat Company

102

and leave it with Stanley. In two weeks time she'll have it looking like new. And just ask any cowboy and he'll tell you a clean old hat beats a new one every time.

The Huskey's Hat Company is located at 1225 E. Scott in Wichita Falls, Zip Code 76303. We provide that in case you would like to mail your hat to have it cleaned like lots of other people. But if you can stop by, and Stanley isn't too busy, you can even get an informal tour of the shop. Closed on Sunday and Monday. 940-767-2071

★ BOB'S BEST BETS ★

There hasn't been a waterfall in Wichita Falls since the flood of 1886 washed it away. So folks there decided to solve that little problem. They built one. Today the **Wichita Falls Waterfall**, a re-creation of the original, faces north on Interstate 44 for everyone to see.

South of Wichita Falls is Archer City. A traffic light in this town had a lot to do with my decision to seek out and tell stories from and about small Texas towns. Remember the movie "The Last Picture Show?" Remember the ever-present blinking yellow light which was sort of a symbol of the slow pace of the little town? Well, that story was about growing up in a small West Texas town like Archer City, and the movie was actually made there, followed by the sequel about 20 years later. I was intrigued by that blinking yellow light and its symbolism and wondered if there were similar stories to be told about other Texas towns. There were. You can visit Archer City and see for yourself.

Plans are underway in Archer City for the restoration of the real-life **Royal Theater** to be renovated and re-opened as a performing arts center. Larry McMurtry, author of "The Last Picture Show," "Lonesome Dove," and many other Texas tomes, is helping revitalize his hometown with a rare and used bookstore called "**Booked Up!**" For more information on Archer City, call 940-574-2489.

Do You Frame It or Sleep In It?

After a lot of years and a lot of miles on the road, sometimes you feel like you just might meet yourself coming back the other way. Often we ask ourselves if we've been here before, done this already. Sometimes we have. That's how it felt when our old friend Bill Richardson wandered up to our booth in the Electra Dairy Queen and offered to show us his steel art.

Now we had already told the world about Bill's steel saddles — leather look illusions too heavy to set on any horse but just perfect for starting conversation. "That," Bill said, "was dysfunctional art, stuff you could only look at. Now I'm doing art with a purpose." Once again we found ourselves sidetracked for the sake of curiosity, traveling down a dirty road detour leading to another chapter in our backroads biographies.

Bill's creativity applies to his storytelling, too.

Bill Richardson spoke the truth. What we found at his remote ranch was what I would have to call "functional fine art." Beds and tables, furniture formed from forgotten freight. Bill had picked through his pastures and rescued things like old wagon wheels and water well parts, things from rusting scrap heaps piled on the prairie. This was once the stuff of someone's dreams, discarded here when it became burdensome.

Now Bill Richardson was making it the stuff of dreams once again, by twisting and torching the hard core steel into functional, "sleepable" art.

It's hard to describe a Bill Richardson Original. Each piece is a one-of-a-kind and he will not and cannot make the exact thing again. His beds may feature a sunflower or a star, a sheriff's badge blown up bigger'n life right there in the center of the headboard. It then becomes the centerpiece of a masterpiece, a piece of furniture and an heirloom to be handed down. Its structure is steel and its character is cowboy. Bill says there is nothing more dangerous than a cowboy with cutting torch. Add to that a wild imagination and a mind wilder than a burlap bag of bobcats and you've got a Bill Richardson original. It takes a special person to turn rusty junk into art. Bill is that person.

If you would like to have a Bill Richardson Original, give him a call at 940-438-2402. And don't try to find his place without a map. Better yet, have Bill meet you at the Electra Dairy Queen. 940-495-2800

"Its structure is steel and its character is cowboy"

★ BOB'S BEST BETS ★

The area around Electra is cattle and oil country. It's wide open and a long way from here to there. West of Electra is Vernon, a town which grew from a cattle-camp on the Western and Dodge Trail. Every October the town hosts the **Greenbelt Fair** with folks coming from the surrounding six counties. Then, during the first weekend of November, they have the **International Barbed Wire and Antique Show**.

Vernon is headquarters of the huge **W.T. Waggoner Ranch**. The **Red River Valley Museum** at 4400 College Drive has a Waggoner Ranch history exhibit and sculpture by Electra Waggoner Biggs. Open Tuesday through Sunday, 1 - 5. 940-553-1848. About 15 miles north of Vernon is **Doan's Crossing**, one of the most famous historic cattle crossings on the Red River.

"Fat-Free" Isn't in Their Vocabulary

Stop #35
Abilene, Texas

"Pure chocolate, pure sugar, Texas peanuts and pecans"

Sometimes it feels like we live in an artificial society complete with simulated flavorings, man-made ingredients and chemical colors. Nothing, it seems, is real anymore. Not so. Come with us to Abilene, Texas.

George Vletas' father came to Abilene in 1912 and opened a business called Olympic Confectionery on Pine Street. Today George still makes candy the old-fashioned way, just like his mother and dad did. He still uses the same copper kettle and same wooden spoons. He still dips the chocolates by hand. And he still uses only real and natural ingredients, making his candy 25 pounds at a time. George says this is the only way he knows and he's not about to change things now. Pure chocolate, pure sugar, Texas peanuts and pecans. Sugar free? Not here. This is the real stuff.

George cooks his candy 25 pounds at a time.

If you're looking for the real stuff, Candies by Vletas is one place to find it. They have lots of different kinds of candy, some things that will be familiar and some you've never seen before. And first time visitors get "grazing rights." Just let Martha Vletas know you're a newcomer and she won't be happy until you've tried several different kinds of candy.

Candies by Vletas is located at 1433 South 14th Street in Abilene. Open Monday through Friday, 9 - 5; Saturday, 10 - 4. 800-752-6933. George and Martha Vletas will be waiting for you.

★ BOB'S BEST BETS ★

Abilene started out as a shipping point for cattle. It was named after Abilene, Kansas, which was the original end point for the famous **Old Chisholm Trail**. When the city celebrated its centennial in 1981, an oil drilling rig was set up on the county fairgrounds just to demonstrate to people that important part of Abilene's economy. By pure accident, the oil demonstration rig struck oil!

Here's an interesting concept: Abilene has several of its museums housed in one location. The old Grace Hotel, built in 1909, is home to the **Arts Museum**, **Historical Museum** and the **Children's Museum**, collectively known as the Museums of Abilene. The building is listed on the National Register of Historic Places. Open Tuesday through Saturday, 10 - 5. Admission fee. On Thursday evenings after 5:00 admission is free and the operating hours are extended until 8:30. 102 Cypress Street. 915-673-4587

Another Abilene building listed on the National Register of Historic Places is the old **Paramount Theater**. This beautiful landmark was built in 1930 in the heart of downtown Abilene and is an excellent example of the grand old theaters of the heyday of Hollywood. The theater's interior is rich in detail. The lobby has arched columns, two grand staircases, hand-blown glass chandeliers, and Pueblo-Deco artwork on the ceiling. The 1,200 seat auditorium features Moorish towers with domed turrets flanking the stage. Slowly drifting clouds and twinkling stars grace the velvet blue ceiling. The theater is used for live performances and classic films. Office hours are from 1 - 5 weekdays and you can stop in for a self-guided tour of the building. 352 Cypress. 915-676-9620

The early days of Abilene are celebrated for ten days in mid-September with the **West Texas Fair**. It features the exhibits, amusements, and attractions of this unique part of the state. In early May, Abilene hosts the **Western Heritage Classic**. The activities include a ranch rodeo, campfire cook-off, sheepdog trials, farrier competition, Cowboy Poet's Society gathering, and Western art show.

Speaking of Buffalo Gap, you should really make a point to visit this historic village with 20 buildings more than 100 years old. All have been restored. They're centered around the first Taylor County Courthouse/Jail. The **Buffalo Gap Historic Village** gives visitors some idea of what it must have been like to have lived here during the days of the founding of this area. 14 miles south of Abilene off FM 89. Hours vary by season. 915-572-3365

Although there are many small towns in Texas boasting various degrees of "revitalization," Baird, located 20 minutes east of Abilene on Interstate 20, is an exceptional example. Within five short years the citizens and business leaders picked themselves up by the bootstraps and brought their historic community from the brink of oblivion to the now official designation of "**Antique Capital of West Texas**." Nowhere else will the antique explorer discover a more colorful and intriguing collection of shops and cafes. The pace, however, is still typical of West Texas: laidback, unhurried, tranquil.

The Callahan County seat has plenty to see and do. The **Old Rock Jail** at 100 West Fifth Street was moved here from the former county seat of Belle Plain. Each block was numbered and the jail was rebuilt exactly the way it had been. Don't be concerned for your safety if you'd like to visit. The most hardened criminals you're likely to run into these days are some rowdy Boy Scouts holding a meeting! Other places of interest include the **Callahan County Pioneer Museum** in the courthouse basement (open Monday through Friday 1 - 5) the **Railroad Heritage Museum** at 100 Market Street (open Monday through Friday 8 - noon) and **Grumpe's Candy Factory** at 206 Market Street, one of only four businesses in the U.S. producing lollipop advertising. For more information on Baird, just stop by the Chamber of Commerce located in the historic 1911 T & P Depot at 100 Market Street or call 915-854-2003.

Art Behind Bars

When you think about prison, nothing very pleasant comes to mind. The best part of a jail is getting out, or so they say. But there's a jail in West Texas where people would actually pay to get in. It's a place where the cells have become cellars and the gallows a gallery. It's the Old Jail Art Center.

When the folks in Albany built a new jail to incarcerate the accused, Albany native Reilly Nail wondered what was to become of the old jail. Why not transform the local clink into a place for Picasso? Today the Old Jail Art Center houses an exceptional collection of permanent art exhibits including the works of Giacomo Manzu, John Marin, Charles Umlauf, Louise Nevelson, Henry Moore, Amedieo Modligliani

Stop #36

Albany, Texas

Just call it the Gray Bar Museum.

and Pablo Picasso. There are also examples of Chinese art from the Han, Wei, Sui, Tang and Ming Dynasties. The old restored county jail offers a research facility for artists, historians, critics and scholars. On Second Street one block east of the courthouse. Open Tuesday through Saturday, 10 - 5; Sunday, 2 - 5. Free admission. 915-762-2269

"Why not transform the local clink into a place for Picasso?"

★ BOB'S BEST BETS ★

A little under 2,000 people call Albany home. It's one of those towns where folks still know each other by name, still gather at the drug store for an ice cream soda. And it's a place where heritage is an important thing, something people want to preserve. That's because lots of folks here can trace their history back to Albany's early settlers. For some, looking at a local history book is like flipping through the pages of a family album. The history of the area is their own. And that's why the folks in Albany fandangle. That's right, fandangle.

It all started back in 1938 when a local author single-handedly wrote all the skits and composed all the songs for a play about Albany and the surrounding area. It's a story filled with all kinds of action - shooting, Indian raids, dancing, fights and flirtations. It's full of humor and sadness, just like real life.

Today nearly 400 folks are part of what's called the **Fort Griffin Fandangle**. In a town the size of Albany that's nearly everyone who can move a set, lift a prop or carry a tune. A local lawyer is the lighting man. A town banker plays guitar and sings. The Church of Christ preacher belts out a song. And they're all volunteers, giving thousands of hours every year to make sure the show goes on. The folks of Albany don't do it for the audience, the applause or cheers. They do it for themselves. They do it for their children. They do it for their town.

You can see a great local production by visiting Albany during the Fort Griffin Fandangle held the last two weekends in June. The annual action-packed production depicting area history is known for its live longhorn, steam train, calliope, overland stage and mule team and a spectacular opening parade of flag bearing riders on horseback. There is a calliope concert and a town barbecue on the courthouse lawn prior to every performance. 915-762-3642 or 915-762-3838

The Cowboy's Calling Card

Long before the MBAs of the world proclaimed the secrets to a successful business are location, location, and location, the Native Americans said, "You have to go where the buffalo are." In his own way, Danny Pollard has gone where the buffalo are.

Danny used to live in the big city, but he decided to make his living as a spur maker. Now I don't know about you, but I don't often see too many people wearing spurs in the big cities, even in Texas. Danny noticed that, too, so he packed up, hit the road and found success in Anson. He says it puts him smack dab in the middle of cowboy country, and cowboys are the ones needing the spurs. Here in his Anson shop, Danny's been cutting, bending, welding and building custom made spurs for several years now. His only lessons in how to make spurs came from the school of trial and error. 445 (give or take a spur or two) satisfied customers later and Danny figures he's just about got it down.

Stop #37

Anson, Texas

Spurs can be practical...and "purty," too!

"From initials to brands to longhorn cattle, he'll find a way to put a custom touch on a West Texas tradition"

Just about anything you want on your spurs Danny can create in silver, brass and steel. From initials to brands to longhorn cattle, he'll find a way to put a custom touch on a West Texas tradition. For cowboys, there is a certain pride in owning a pair of custom-fit and handmade spurs. Truth is, one pair of spurs works about as well as the other, but custom spurs give a cowboy something to show off and brag about, and that's an important part of being a cowboy! Danny could hire help and turn out spurs faster and cheaper, but he says he'll quit before he opens a spur making assembly line. Call it good old Texas pride. Danny calls it quality.

You can have a pair of Danny Pollard spurs or even some of his new ranch-style iron furniture, but you'll have to wait a while. Quality takes time. Danny's shop is 16 miles southwest of Anson. Call 915-823-2429 for directions.

★ BOB'S BEST BETS ★

There ain't no dancin' in Anson. At least not very often. In fact, dancing in this West Texas town was banned, illegal until very recently. No one is sure just how it became illegal to dance in Anson, but there are several explanations depending on which local you ask. One fellow told us during a visit a few years ago that cowboys used to come into town looking for a good time and "busted up the place" when they had too much to drink. Often this took place in local bars and dance halls, so they just banned the dancing. Probably a more accurate explanation is that this is the Bible Belt and some folks felt dancing was wrong for religious reasons. Anyway, there was in fact a town ordinance until about five years ago making it against the law to shake a leg in dancing except for one particular time of year.

For three days each December, usually the weekend before Christmas, Anson hosts the **Cowboys Christmas Ball**. It's a tradition that started in 1885 when cowboys were invited to come to town dressed in their Sunday best and celebrate the season.

The Cowboys Christmas Ball is held every year in **Pioneer Hall**, a rock building built specially for the event. The event was popularized by country singer Michael Martin Murphey's musical rendition of a poem written by rancher Larry Chittenden after attending the ball in 1890. For information on the ball, contact the Anson Chamber of Commerce at 915-823-3259. Be advised that the Cowboys Christmas Ball is always a sell-out and reservations are required well in advance.

If you can't make the ball, visit the local post office and see the **Depression-era mural** painted on the wall there. When it was unveiled in the 30s, some of the local townsfolk became angry because it depicted a scene from the annual Cowboys Christmas Ball and showed people dancing, which was, of course, illegal.

North of Anson is Stamford, famous for its annual **Texas Cowboy Reunion**. The population of this tiny town triples every year around July 4th, when more than 500 rodeo contestants and thousands of spectators converge for the three-day event. It all began in 1930 as a non-profit community enterprise, and is said to be unchallenged as the greatest amateur rodeo in the world. The festivities include chuckwagon meals and a Western art show.

While you're in Stamford, be sure to check out the **Mackenzie Trail Monument**. This large hand-carved marker was erected by the descendants of early ranchers and summarizes the importance of a major pioneer route along the present intersection of US 277 and Texas 6 North. 915-773-2411

"There ain't no dancin' in Anson. At least not very often."

The Bat Lady

Stop #38

Mineral Wells, Texas

You probably grew up thinking the same thing about bats that I did. That they were dangerous little blood-sucking creatures that chased people down and bit them. That they were mean and vicious and had little regard for people. Guess what. I'm now trying to get some bats to come live at my house, and it's all because of Amanda Lollar.

Amanda Lollar called me one day and asked me to stop by her place in Mineral Wells to see what she was doing with an animal she had rescued in front of her furniture store. She wouldn't tell me what it was, only that it was a mammal. Couldn't be that weird, I thought, so I dropped by while I was traveling the area. In a matter of minutes, I was in love with bats. Amanda explained that she quite literally stumbled onto this helpless little creature in front of the family business and couldn't leave it there to die, even though she was repulsed by bats. As she nursed it back to health, she learned a lot about bats.

When I visited Amanda and her bats a few years ago, she showed me places in the old Baker Hotel (see more under Best Bets below) where the creatures would try to make a home and get trapped. I went with her to rescue several bats. Then we went to her

Amanda rescues bats from the old Baker Hotel.

114

furniture store where she and the bats lived in the back. Today, the family furniture business has given way to Bat World Sanctuary and Educational Center, providing a lifetime home, in natural habitat setting, to permanently injured bats, bats used in research and those confiscated from the illegal pet trade. Besides offering visitors a unique view of these fascinating and misunderstood creatures, Bat World provides medical attention, rescue and release for hundreds of bats each year. Amanda has more than 100 bats representing 12 species from all over the world and the only non-releasable bat sanctuary anywhere for sick and orphaned bats.

Bat World is at 217 North Oak Avenue and is open for public tours only on the second Saturday and third Sunday of each month September through June. Amanda asks that you call ahead to reserve your tour. Admission fee. 940-325-3404

"In a matter of minutes, I was in love with bats"

★ BOB'S BEST BETS ★

There was a time when Mineral Wells was famous nationwide, mostly because of the **Baker Hotel**. This grand hotel played host to such celebrities as Jack Dempsey, Jean Harlowe, Marlene Dietrich, Clark Gable, Judy Garland and my favorite, the Three Stooges! At one time, Mineral Wells was famous because of the medicinal qualities in the water, called Crazy Water after a well was discovered in 1885. People traveled to Mineral Wells to soak themselves in baths of the water at places like the Baker Hotel. The old hotel was designed after the Arlington Hotel in Hot Springs, Arkansas. The 14-story structure is 180 feet tall and has 450 rooms over 250,000 square feet. Though the hotel closed in 1972 after people realized the water really did not cure them of mental illness or constipation, you can still re-live some of its grandeur by visiting some of the businesses now housed downstairs. For more information, call 800-252-MWTX or 940-325-2557.

Exit at the XIT

Stop #39

Dalhart, Texas

They called it the XIT. Back when Texas was still young and untamed, it took 6,000 miles of prickly steel barbed wire to fence her in and the ranch covered 10 counties in the Texas Panhandle. It was 27 miles wide and over 200 miles long. Seems the State of Texas wanted to build a new capitol building in Austin, but didn't want to spend the money to do it, so they made a trade with some Chicago folks: You build our magnificent building and we'll give you 3,000,000 acres of prime real estate in Northwest Texas. The result was the world's largest ranch!

The ranch operated its own stores and schools, and entire towns sprung up within its boundaries. It was so big that it was too big. Cattle rustlers and the enormous size did in the XIT and it was broken into "little parcels" of 150,000 to 250,000 acres and sold. Still, the XIT touched a lot of lives for a lot of years, and folks still come back to the Panhandle town of

A weekend filled with memories and cowboy tradition

116

Dalhart every summer to honor her. The event began as an actual reunion of cowboys and their families — folks who grew up and worked on the XIT. It has evolved into the XIT Rodeo and Reunion, which is quite an event with parades, races, booths, arts, crafts and, of course, a rodeo.

There's lots of free food at this event, too, with the Free Stew Feed on Thursday night and the Free Watermelon Feed on Friday. On Saturday afternoon, they dig up the world's biggest brisket and offer up food for 20,000 or more at the World's Largest Free Barbecue! This thing is so big they actually use bulldozers to bury the meat underground where it cooks for at least 24 hours.

The XIT Rodeo and Reunion is held in Dalhart every year on the first Thursday, Friday and Saturday in August. There is an admission charge for special events like the rodeo and dance. 806-249-5646

"It was so big that it was too big"

★ BOB'S BEST BETS ★

Even if you don't go to Dalhart during the XIT Rodeo and Reunion, be sure to visit the **XIT Museum** at 108 East Fifth Street. Open Tuesday through Saturday, 9 - 5. Free admission. 806-249-5390.

There is a traffic island in Dalhart that tells more of the XIT story at something called the **Empty Saddle Monument**. As the story goes, there was an XIT cowboy who died just before the annual reunion. His widow asked that a horse be allowed to participate in the parade without the cowboy, thus, the monument and the tradition of a saddled horse without a rider every year in the parade.

About 30 miles south of Dalhart off US 385 in Old Tascosa there is a home for kids called **Cal Farley's Boys Ranch**. Young boys who need extra help growing up come here to live and go to school. They also work on the ranch where they grow their own food, cattle, and even operate their own dairy. Cal Farley's Boys Ranch is open to visitors who would like to see how this place is run. 800-687-3722

The Old West Meets
The Old Country

Okay, let's admit it. We Texans can be brash and bold and bragging. In fact, some of our culture is defined by that kind of behavior. Most of the time those who engage in this kind of activity do it because they know people expect it of us. If you come all the way from Germany to Texas, you want to see men wearing boots and hats. You want to see big ranches with oil wells and you want to see big Texans bragging.

There is a place in Amarillo where you won't be disappointed if all that Texas stuff is what you're looking for. It's called the Big Texan Steak Ranch and it's right there on the highway not far from the airport. You'll know it by the sign which boldly announces that

His name may be Ed Montana, but this cowboy's all Texan.

anyone who can eat a 72-ounce steak in one hour can have it for free. For those who cannot finish off this hunk of cow in the allotted 60 minutes, bank financing is available! This is the place where you want to take your relatives from New England. Once again, they expect it of us. We have to live up to our image.

But aside from its world famous 72-ounce side-of-beef, the Big Texan has become famous for something else. Something that goes down a lot easier. Ed Montana.

Ed Montana is one of those big Texans who can pick a guitar and yodel a tune with the best of 'em, just the way people expect. As he puts it, the world's not through with the Wild West yet, and that's part of the reason for the success of the Big Texan, a place with more yee-haws per square yard than a John Wayne Western. And that's part of the reason for the success of Ed's music... in places as far away as Austria!

Seems Europeans have a thing for Texas and the Old West and Ed has found a way to give it to them. Every year he travels to the pubs and clubs of the old country to perform real cowboy music. They line up and pack in to see Ed. Then, some of them follow him all the way back home. Home to Amarillo where they get to take part in a real cowboy round-up, gettin' little dogies along and all that. This cowboy crooner has become a big hit with our European friends.

Ed Montana offers up some great listening pleasure. He plays pretty regularly at the Big Texan and Country Barn in Amarillo, and you can also catch him at some of the rodeos in Texas. Ed works for the local Coors Beer Distributor, and if you call them at 806-376-5674, they'll be glad to help you get a performance schedule. The Big Texan Steak Ranch is located at 7701 I-40 East.

"This cowboy crooner has become a big hit with our European friends"

★ BOB'S BEST BETS ★

Another thing we Texans are known for is our quarter horses and Amarillo is home to the **American Quarter Horse Heritage Center and Museum**.

They have a registry of more than 2.6 million horses here, the world's largest equine registry. The quarter horse was the first American horse breed and still the favorite mount among cowboys. From May to Labor Day, the museum and gift shop are open Monday through Saturday, 9 - 5; September to April, Tuesday through Saturday, 10 - 5. Admission fee. Interstate 40 at Quarter Horse Drive (exit 72A). 806-376-5181

One of the most eccentric Texans is a man named Stanley Marsh. Among all the stunts he's pulled over the years, the **Cadillac Ranch** has to be the strangest. On I-40 just west of Amarillo you'll see 10 vintage 1949-1963 Cadillacs buried nose down in a field at the same angle as Cheop's pyramids. Nobody knows why Stanley did this, but over the past 20 years it's made for some great conversation. You can walk out to the cars for picture taking and sometimes you can even sign your name to one of the vehicles. Free admission.

If you want to see some great scenery and experience a little bit of cowboy life at the same time, take in one of the chuckwagon breakfasts offered at Amarillo area ranches. Tom Christian owns a ranch 27 miles from Amarillo and grew up here raising cattle. Tom's **Cowboy Morning** offers a great breakfast on the edge of Palo Duro Canyon from April through October. Cowboy Morning is also Cowboy Evening. They now serve steak dinners with all the trimmings. They have good scrambled eggs and sourdough biscuits and even better conversation. Call 800-658-2613 for scheduling information.

Nearby in Canyon, Texas, is an outdoor musical drama called **"TEXAS"** which tells the story of this area in song and dance. It's performed in a natural amphitheater in Palo Duro Canyon by professional dancers and actors, local residents and students from West Texas A & M University. Nearly 3 million people from every state and more than 100 countries have seen this production, rated one of the Top 100 Attractions in North America by the American Bus Association. There is a barbecue supper served before the play and some great entertainment by some friends of ours called The Prairie Dogs. "TEXAS" is performed every night at 8:30 from mid-June through mid-August. Reserved tickets are encouraged. 806-655-2181

The "TEXAS" production is famous for its music and action.

Visit five museums in one at the **Panhandle-Plains Historical Museum** in Canyon. Sections of this more than 60-year-old facility are devoted to petroleum, transportation, and art. Exhibits include a gun collection, pre-historic fossils, and Native American cultures, archaeology, and the **Frank Reaugh Collection of Southwestern Art**. If you've been bitten by the history bug, check out the museum's research center complete with records and photographs documenting the history of the Panhandle and Southwest. It's all on the West Texas A & M Campus and is open Monday through Saturday, 9 - 5 (until 6 June - August) Sunday 1 - 6. Admission is free, but donations are appreciated. 806-656-2244

One of several **Texas Travel Information Centers** throughout the state is located in Amarillo. It's at the intersection of Interstate 40 and US 287 just east of the city. Tourists can learn more about the Lone Star State from professional travel counselors providing maps, literature, and route advice.

'Til The Cows Come Home

Stop #41
Miami, Texas

"It's one of the strangest... and loudest... gatherings in the entire state"

There are lots of fairs and festivals in Texas. Some of them exist just because someone was looking for something catchy and cute to name a festival so folks would visit their town (Marshall's Fire Ant Festival) while others are rooted in local history, customs or business (Poteet's Strawberry Festival). There are practical reasons for lots of festivals (San Antonio's River Walk Mud Festival takes advantage of the annual draining and cleaning of the channel) and some have so much history they have taken on a life of their own perhaps even bigger than their host town (Canton's First Monday Trade Days). But Miami, Texas, is the only town in Texas that built a festival around the art of hollerin'.

It's called the Miami National Cow Calling Championship. It's a kind of homecoming celebration for this panhandle town where old-timers meet newcomers and catch up with other old-timers. It's a legitimate reason for folks to get together and scream at the top of their lungs. It's one of the strangest... and loudest... gatherings in the entire state. It's a chance to see who's the best at calling Old Bessie home.

Before we go any further we need to get one thing straight. This town is not My-am-ee like that place in Florida, even though it's spelled the same. It's My-am-uh, with the emphasis on the am part. My-AM-uh. It's

"Hi-oooooooh-dees! Hey Cow!"

an Indian word meaning "sweetheart," or something close to that.

What they do at the Miami National Cow Calling Championship is just that - call cows. The only hitch is there's not a cow in sight, or even within hearing distance, so they're not really calling cows. It's more of a screamin' or hollerin' contest, since you can yell as loud as you want all day and no cows will come. The entries come from all over the state, even from other states, and the styles of hollerin' vary from simple "woop-woop-woops" to "Hi-oooooooh-dees" to "Owwwwwww-AHHHHHHHHH-deeeeeeeeees" to "Hey, Cow!"

The Miami National Cow Calling Championship is held every year on the first Saturday of June. There is no charge to enter the festival, only for the barbecue. Maybe that's what happened to the cows. 806-868-3721

★ BOB'S BEST BETS ★

Miami originated as a construction camp on the Santa Fe Railroad. It is fitting, then, that the **Roberts County Museum** is housed in an old Santa Fe Depot at the corner of Commercial and Mobeetie. The collection at this museum includes such things as household items, a half-dugout and lots of Indian relics. Open Tuesday through Friday 10 - 5. Admission is free. 806-868-3291

West of Miami in southern Hutchinson County is **Borger**. This is a relatively new Texas town and was founded when oil was discovered in 1926. In a matter of months more than 40,000 people were living in tents and shacks. When Borger was just three years old, state guardsmen moved in to clean up the town and clear out the "undesirables." Then a group of the town's businessmen worked to completely redesign and landscape their downtown. Today, the population numbers 17,000 and there are 26 parks in this once bawdy boomtown.

A Texas Time Warp

Stop #42
Dimmitt, Texas

"One day Reavis Kerr locked the door and never went back"

Most of us have at least given thought, at some point in our lives, to changing everything about our lives. Maybe you've thought of "starting over" in a different direction, or perhaps you've entertained the idea of just walking away from whatever you do for a living and never going back. In Dimmitt, Texas, someone did just that. Just left and never went back.

Reavis Kerr had a hardware store in downtown Dimmitt. Kerr Hardware was a fixture among other little shops right there at 203 E. Bedford Street. Then, one day, Reavis Kerr gave it all up. But he didn't run an ad in the local newspaper and sell his store. He didn't even liquidate his merchandise and pay off his mortgage or lease. He just walked away. That's right, one day Reavis Kerr locked the door and never went back. And everything Reavis Kerr had for sale in his store that day is still there.

Look through the window and you'll see the Radio Flyer bicycles lined up just like they were when Mr. Kerr locked the door. The shelves are lined with items priced to sell. The calendar on the wall is still hanging open to March 1956, to the very day over 40 years ago when Reavis Kerr gave it all up. And no one, except Mr. Kerr, knows why.

Local lore is that Mr. Kerr disappeared after he locked his store and was never heard from again. That's not exactly true. I tracked him down back in the early 80s and asked him why he did it. He was very nice, talked to me on the phone for several minutes, but when I asked the question we all are dying to know, Mr. Kerr's answer was, "It just seemed like the thing to do." Whatever. After all, it's his store. And if he suddenly decided to open it up again, that would be his business, too. In the meantime, stop by, clean off a spot on the plate glass window and take a peek inside. This is something you probably will never see again.

There's not much more anyone can tell you, but for more information you can contact the Dimmitt Chamber of Commerce at 806-647-2524.

Memories for sale at Kerr Hardware

★ BOB'S BEST BETS ★

For several years, Sam Raper and Sam Raper, Jr. were a combination of father and son art team and two-man clean-up crew for Dimmitt. Folks in Dimmitt knew when they saw a gold station wagon flying around town, it was none other than the two Sams on the hunt again for bottlecaps. They took their bottle tops home and turned them into... what else? **Bottle Cap Sculpture.** Even though at this writing Sam Sr. is in poor health and can no longer create art from bottlecaps, you can still see some of the Rapers' work at the Castro County Museum where three pieces remain on display. 404 W. Halsell. Open Monday through Friday, 1 - 5. Admission is free. 806-647-2611

North of Dimmitt, just south of Hereford, is the site

of a WWII prisoner of war camp. Officially called the **Hereford Military Reservation and Reception Center**, the POW camp covered 800 acres in northern Castro County. It was "home" to 7,000 Italian prisoners of war and 1,000 American soldiers. Then, in mid-1945, in the final days of the war, the Italian prisoners asked for and received permission to build a monument to the five POWs who died at the camp. A prayer chapel was erected at the prisoners' burial ground near the camp. It was a 13' by 13' structure which the POWs built mostly by hand, using their own money to buy materials. Even though they had no machinery to help with their construction, the prisoners built a beautiful monument with interior plaster walls that looked like granite and an altar that looked like marble.

Over the years the site was vandalized, but a few years ago local residents refurbished the POW prayer chapel and historical markers were put in place. In 1989 the restoration project was completed and the little POW chapel was formally dedicated, with former POWs returning to the site from Italy to take part in the ceremony. The chapel is enclosed by a high protective fence made of four-point barbed wire from the original camp. Two flagpoles stand in front of the structure - one for the United States flag and one for the flag of Italy.

You can visit this site by taking Highway 385 south from Hereford approximately 1 1/4 miles. Turn right on FM 1055. Go about three miles on CR 1. One mile later, turn left on an unmarked road. Go 1/3 mile and the chapel is on the right side of the road. From Dimmitt, take Highway 385 north seven miles. Turn left on FM 2397. Go six miles and then turn right on FM 1055. Go 7 miles and turn left on CR 1. Go one mile and turn left on an unmarked road. 1/3 mile later, the chapel is on the right side of the road. Keep in mind that the chapel is locked. If you'd like to do more than look through the windows, call Clara Vick ahead of time at 806-647-3154.

Something Wild In Muleshoe

Don Clapp says some folks might call the area around Muleshoe, Texas, bleak. It's pretty much one or two shades of color a lot of the time - light brown and darker brown. But if you like open spaces and nature, he says this is the place to be. "We get people who drive in off the highway and expect to see animals like you would in a zoo," Don says. "Then they say, 'There's nothing out here to see' and they're on their way."

Along with a camera and a picnic lunch, visitors to the Muleshoe National Wildlife Refuge need to pack a generous supply... of patience. You see, this ain't no pettin' zoo. It's the High Plains of West Texas, and folks out to sneak a peek at the wild have to do it on nature's own terms.

One type of creature you might see at the Muleshoe Wildlife Refuge is the sandhill crane. Every year, just like clockwork, thousands of these beautiful winged creatures descend upon Muleshoe to winter on the refuge. The shallow lakes here are a welcome sight to the weary cranes who are ending a 3,000 mile non-stop journey from their homes in Canada, Alaska and even

Stop #43

Muleshoe, Texas

Don's always on the look-out for cranes.

parts of Siberia. To some people in Muleshoe the return of the cranes is as much a herald of the changing seasons as the turning fall leaves. To others, it symbolizes nature in all her mystery and wonder. But to Don Clapp, the cranes represent a kind of untamed beauty that he's called to cherish and protect. In Muleshoe they like to say it was the mule that tamed the old west. Don Clapp says it's the crane that keeps her wild.

The sandhill cranes normally begin arriving around the end of September. For the next 6 months this area hosts the largest concentration of sandhill cranes in North America, with the number of cranes at the refuge reaching its peak between December and mid-February.

The Muleshoe National Wildlife Refuge is located 20 miles south of Muleshoe, Texas, on State Highway 214. Open Monday through Friday 8 - 4:30. Free admission. 806-946-3341

★ BOB'S BEST BETS ★

If your town is named Muleshoe it makes sense there would be a mule memorial and this town's got a good one. The **National Mule Memorial** was built by a group of Texans who were determined to erect a monument to the unsung mule. The memorial is at the intersection of U.S. 70/84 in downtown Muleshoe. 806-272-4248

It may seem a strange suggestion, but you might want to find a place to watch television while you're visiting Muleshoe. Magann Lamb Rennels is the owner and operator of the local cable news show. Her father was a local radio personality for many years, and when cable television became popular, it was just natural for the family to carry the tradition to the tube. Magann broadcasts from a room in her home and whatever happens to be going on at the Rennels house is what you will see on television. After seeing Muleshoe's **Channel 17**, some of the phony sticky sweet slick stuff you see on television these days probably won't appeal to you!

Old McDonald Had...
Just About Everything!

Pete McDonald founded his business during the Great Depression. He says he can't remember exactly how much start-up money it took to open the doors, but he knows it wasn't even as much as a hundred dollars because that was enough to buy the whole county back then, and if he could've he would've!

McDonald's Trading Post rises out of the plains like a big yellow beacon to the bargain hunter - 60,000 square feet of floor space spread over 15 acres, 6 city blocks and two streets of Plainview, Texas. At McDonald's Trading Post they have a slogan: "If we don't have it, you don't need it." They also say it's the "Home of a Million Items." We weren't about to start counting, so we decided to take Pete's word for it - Pete's NEVER been known to stretch the truth - and if you believe that, he's got some ocean front property in Plainview to sell you! Call him a character or a cut-up, but Pete is a person you won't soon forget.

"There's all kinds of people in this world," Pete told us. "I know I'm not the only nut."

He's a junk dealer, a trader, fixer and part-time marriage counselor. He says if he can't reconcile 'em he'll buy 'em out cheap. He says he deals with dreamers, builders, jackleg mechanics and do-it-yourselfers. He admits he overcharges some of 'em, but only so he can pass the savings on to you.

Bottom line is you can't beat the bottom line deals at McDonald's. You can buy 100,000-pound scales, practice bombs and all the parking meters you can carry. There's wheels and pumps and motors and tires and "things too numerous to mention — mostly numerous." All that and you get a Vegas caliber comedy show thrown in free o' charge. But there is one subject that for Pete is no laughing matter. That's the correct description for his long and lengthy line of goods - Pete's life work.

"I buy junk, but I sell merchandise," he told us. "My wife tells me that I've buried myself and created

Stop #44
Plainview, Texas

"At McDonald's Trading Post they have a slogan: If we don't have it, you don't need it"

The sales pitch alone is worth a trading post trip.

a monstrosity. And she may be right about that."

McDonald's Trading Post is located at 1401 South Columbia Street in Plainview. Open Monday through Friday, 8 - 6; Saturday, 8 - 1. Pete has four golf carts to make your shopping easier. Just ask for the keys at the store. 806-296-9239

★ BOB'S BEST BETS ★

Due east of Plainview is the town of Turkey. This town is probably best known as the birthplace of favorite son Bob Wills, the founder of the music known as Western Swing, a mixture of big band, jazz, blues and country music. Bob Wills died in 1975, but his music still brings thousands of devotees to Turkey every year for **Bob Wills Day**, which has actually become three or four days. There are fiddlers' contests, dances and performances by remaining members of Bob Wills' band, the Texas Playboys. The festival is held the last weekend in April. 806-423-1151

South Plains Snow Birds

Every year, echoes of winter wing southward across the plowed pastures and planted fields of the Texas high plains. Millions of Canada geese fly to the south, sounding the call of cold weather in West Texas. Geese move in for the winter like they have for hundreds of years, thousands of miles from their remote summer nesting grounds in far removed regions of the Arctic. But one spot is becoming increasingly popular among the geese. They've selected Lubbock, Texas, as their preferred wintering grounds. Scientists are baffled as to why every year thousands more crowd their way into Lubbock. This town may not be paradise in the winter, but one thing is certain - the hub city of the South Plains is host to one of the largest populations of visiting Canada geese anywhere in North America.

To some, this scenario provides the ultimate contradiction. After all, we tend to think of wildlife, especially those originating in the natural wonderlands of the far reaches of North America, as preferring

Stop #45
Lubbock, Texas

Honk if you love geese!

picturesque, lush landscapes with a minimum of human interference. Lubbock is a lot of things, but it is not that. It is a vibrant, busy city with a great deal to offer, but there isn't a forest in sight. Obviously, the Canada geese don't mind. Every fall they move in on the local city park waterfowl, crowding the shorelines anywhere there is water, huddled defiantly against the cold.

You can witness the beauty of the Canada geese in Lubbock. There is a year-round population which has taken up permanent residency on the South Plains, but the first cold front each year brings with it thousands of migrating Canada geese. There are three primary viewing spots. Lake Ransom Canyon on Highway 835 east of Lubbock hosts the largest population. If you will drive to this location about sunrise, the sky will be clouded with the geese as they move to area fields for their morning feeding, filling the air with their familiar honking sound as they do. Inside the city, Leroy Elmore Park at South Quaker and Loop 289, and Maxey Park at Quaker and 19th Street each have large numbers of Canada geese. The birds are very friendly and appreciate it if you'll stop at a local feed store and pick up some corn for their enjoyment!

★ BOB'S BEST BETS ★

If it's wildlife you love, visit **Mackenzie Park** near the fairgrounds in east Lubbock. This 500 acre park is home to **Prairie Dog Town** where some of the friendliest, and fattest, prairie dogs in all of West Texas reside. This particular population has enjoyed so many years of tourism that they have become somewhat portly on a diet of marshmallows tossed by well-meaning visitors.

West Texas has been home to some giants in the music industry, and the **Buddy Holly Statue and Walk of Fame** honors Lubbock and West Texas natives who made significant contributions to entertainment. Plaques include Mac Davis, Waylon

Jennings, Jimmy Dean, Buddy Holly's band "The Crickets" and others. There is a bronze statue of Lubbock's favorite son Buddy Holly that stands 8'6" tall and weighs 2500 pounds in front of the Lubbock Memorial Civic Center at 8th and Avenue Q.

Lubbock has become quite a center of the growing Texas wine industry with two of the state's finest wineries here. **Cap Rock Winery** on U.S. Hwy. 87 South and Woodrow Road is in a beautiful mission-style building and is open Monday through Saturday 10 - 5, Sundays noon - 5. Admission is free. 806-863-2704. **Llano Estacado Winery** is Texas' most award winning winery using grapes grown within a 60-mile radius of Lubbock. Located south of town on FM 1585. Open Monday through Saturday 10 - 5, Sundays noon - 5. Free admission and tours. 806-745-2258

If you're looking for a step back in time to the days of the Old West, Lubbock is just the place to find it. The **Ranching Heritage Center** at 4th St. and Indiana offers visitors a hands-on experience of the taste, touch and feel of early ranch life. Exhibits at the center include 33 historic ranch buildings that have been relocated to this 14-acre site. Open Tuesday through Sunday 10 - 5. Free admission. 806-742-2442

Soon, the **National Windmill Project** will be moved from its building site in a Lubbock warehouse

The vanishing symbol of the pioneer spirit

to a facility on the Texas Tech campus. When it is complete, visitors will be able to stroll through the largest collection of wind machines anywhere. The project was the dream of the late Billie Wolfe who began collecting the windmills some 30 years ago. This retired home economics professor began her work after noticing that windmills were disappearing from Southern homes. She then began gathering photographs, historical documents and finally windmills themselves in an effort to preserve the legacy of these pinwheels of the prairie. Billie even outbid the Smithsonian Institute in her goal of becoming the world's leading windmill collector. Call 806-788-1499 if you're interested in a tour.

One of the most interesting sites in this town is the **Lubbock Lake Landmark State Historical Park**. It is the only known site in North America that contains deposits related to cultures existing on the Southern Plains over the last 12,000 years. This national historic landmark has yielded evidence of ancient peoples and extinct animals. During the summertime, visitors can participate in actual archaeological digs. If you're interested, it's best to call ahead. The **Robert Nash Interpretive Center** includes exhibits, a gallery and a children's learning laboratory. Small admission fee. 2200 North Landmark Drive. 806-741-0306

Every September, Lubbock plays host to the largest American presentation of ranching, cowboys, and the Western way of life. The **National Cowboy Symposium** draws poets, musicians, storytellers, artists, historians, authors, editors, publishers, photographers, cooks, and honest-to-goodness cowboys from across the country. Highlights include a horse parade to kick off the event, the **American Cowboy Culture Awards Show**, and the **National Championship Chuckwagon Cookoff**. Most activities are held at the Lubbock Memorial Civic Center and adjacent grounds at 1501 6th St. Free horse-drawn carriage rides are offered between Civic Center locations. Admission fee. 806-795-2455

The Ghost Of The Texas Grill

The folks at the Ballinger Chamber of Commerce probably aren't going to like this, but Ballinger is a ghost town. No, it's not full of abandoned buildings. There are no tumbleweeds blowing down Main Street. In fact, Ballinger is a vibrant, energetic West Texas town with a lot to offer. But that doesn't change things. Lots of folks say a ghost lives here, right there inside a building on Highway 83 at the Texas Grill.

Highway 83 is a long, lonely, ribbon of blacktop that cuts across the United States like a snake trail running from Canada to Mexico. Scattered along the way are literally hundreds of greasy spoon cafes, interesting characters and roadside haunts. But nothing on Highway 83 is quite like the Texas Grill in Ballinger.

Larry Sikes grew up behind the counter at the Texas Grill, met his wife Joyce here, and now the three of them own this place. That's right, the three of them - Larry, Joyce and the ghost of the Texas Grill.

Employees and customers alike have heard creaks, groans and footsteps upstairs. It's been going on for about as long as anyone around here can remember. Folks used to just call "it" the ghost, but that was before someone in Ballinger got the bright idea of holding a seance to try and talk to the ghost one-on-one. According to local lore, the spirit told everyone at the seance that he was from the neighboring town of Norton. From then on, the ghost had a name - Norton.

Norton stays active and likes to make a lot of noise. And he likes to sneak around, letting you catch site of him as he moves from room to room. Then, when you investigate, no one is there. When folks say history is alive in Ballinger, they really mean it. Until recently, the story of Norton was nothing more than a lot of talk and a lot of tales. But that was before Wendy Scivener decided to take party pictures at the annual Christmas party. When the film came back from being developed and printed, there was old Norton right there in Wendy's party pics. Talk about a photo opportunity! Seems Norton doesn't miss a trick!

Like we said, the folks at the local chamber may not

Stop #46
Ballinger, Texas

"There's something stirring in the kitchen other than cream gravy"

like it, but Ballinger is a ghost town. At least Joyce and Larry Sikes think so. They'll be the first to tell you there's something stirring in the kitchen other than cream gravy. But that's okay, it's just Norton, the ghost of the Texas Grill.

The Texas Grill is located at 700 Hutchings in Ballinger. Open Monday through Wednesday 5 am - 10 pm, Thursdays and Sundays until 11 pm and Fridays and Saturdays they're open around the clock. 915-365-3314

The "old haunt" of Ballinger, Texas

★ BOB'S BEST BETS ★

Ballinger claims to be "The Greatest Little Town in Texas" and we won't dispute that. Folks from out of state who visit this town expecting to see the typical West Texas sand and sagebrush will soon discover they're all wet. Ballinger was built along the Colorado River and nearby **Lake Ivie** provides the town with prime water activities. The legendary fishing along with boating, hiking and camping bring lots of tourists to Ballinger. That combined with low humidity and an average annual temperature of 78 degrees makes this town one of the top attractions in this part of the state.

Anyone who has driven near Ballinger, especially at night, has noticed and no doubt wondered about "**The Cross**." It stands on a hill south of town off of the Paint Rock Highway. The iron cross weighs about 100,000 pounds and stands 100 feet tall and 70 feet across. Jim and Doris Studer had the giant cross placed on their property as a tribute to God. It can be seen for miles around. The cross is illuminated and is especially noticeable at night. You may visit the cross between the hours of 9 and 5 daily, but it is actually best appreciated from a distance.

One of the longest titled festivals in Texas takes place on the largest landscaped courthouse lawn in Texas. The last weekend of each April is always set aside in Ballinger for the **Texas State Festival of Ethnic Cultures and Arts and Crafts Show** (whew!) There is a large parade, the crowning of "Miss Ballinger," ethnic food booths and lots of arts and crafts displays. There is also a big dance on Saturday night which always features "name" entertainment.

Ballinger's **Carnegie Library** building is one of 34 library buildings funded by the philanthropist Andrew Carnegie. It is one of only four of those buildings which is still being used as a public library. The building was restored inside and out in the 70s and 80s and is well worth a visit.

Just north of Ballinger is **Winters**, which could have a dispute with Ballinger if not for one word. While Ballinger claims to be the "Greatest Little Town in Texas," Winters makes claim to the title "The Best Little Town in Texas." So far there have been no altercations between citizens of Ballinger and Winters over the Best and Greatest Little Towns in the state!

Old Warbirds Never Die

They stand stoically at attention in a shiny, new hangar in Midland, Texas. Retired soldiers, war torn but battle ready. Fifty years have come and gone since the skies over Europe were filled with the thunder of their mighty engines. But old soldiers and old memories never die. And some of the men who rode these huge hunks of metal to victory are trying to make sure they never ever fade away.

The Confederate Air Force/American Airpower Heritage Museum is dedicated to the acquisition, restoration and preservation in flying condition of vintage military aircraft from World War II. It all started after the war when a handful of former service pilots put their wartime flying experience to use as crop duster pilots in Texas' Lower Rio Grande Valley. A group of them purchased a surplus P-51 Mustang in 1957 and set an idea in motion. The seed had been planted for the growth of the nation's finest collection of flyable WW II combat aircraft. What these dedicated pilots soon discovered is that virtually all of the nearly 300,000 aircraft produced during the war had been destroyed. They vowed to try to preserve at least one of each type so that future generations would understand and appreciate the importance and accomplishments of American airpower.

Stop #47

Midland, Texas

Old airships fly again in Midland.

Today the museum has an impressive collection of aircraft from the U.S., Britain, Germany and Japan. At least 20 of the 137 planes in the CAF are on display at any one time with different aircraft shown every three months. The P-40 Warhawk, P-38 Lightning, P-47 Thunderbolt and lots of other flyable planes are in the collection.

The museum is open Monday through Saturday 9 - 5, Sundays and holidays noon - 5. Located at Midland International Airport 8 miles west of I-20. Admission fee. 915-563-1000

★ BOB'S BEST BETS ★

When in Midland the first thing you'll notice is that you're in oil country. Pumpjacks are everywhere and the city recognizes and honors the oil industry and the history of the area at the **Permian Basin Petroleum Museum, Library and Hall of Fame**. On exhibit are such items as reed mats and woven fiber articles from the area's prehistoric population, cowboy tack, early railroad artifacts and early oil boomtown paintings and photographs. Open Monday through Saturday 9 - 5, Sunday 2 - 5 at 1500 I-20 West. Admission fee. 915-683-4403

Twenty miles west of Midland is its sister city Odessa. If you think Midland-Odessa is just a rough and rugged oil area, think again. Odessa is home to the **Globe of the Great Southwest** at 2308 Shakespeare Road on the Odessa College Campus. This theater is a replica of the Globe Theater in London, and like its English counterpart, was built specifically to host only plays by William Shakespeare. Tours are given by appointment only, but performances go on year-round. Call 915-332-1586 for information.

Another "only" found in Odessa is the **Presidential Museum**, which is the only facility anywhere dedicated solely to the office of the U.S. presidency. This museum is open Tuesday through Saturday 10 - 5. 622 North Lee Street. Admission is free. 915-332-7123

"The men who rode these hunks of metal to victory are making sure they never fade away"

The Real Life Rosa's Cantina

"Out in the West Texas town of El Paso
I fell in love with a Mexican girl
Nighttime would find me in Rosa's Cantina
Music would play and Faleena would whirl"

It's what songwriters call a perfect fit. The southernmost tip of the Rocky Mountains, the Rio Grande river, and an obscure landmark - a place called Rosa's Cantina.

Roberto Zubia and his wife Anita opened this simple eatery almost 40 years ago along what was then Highway 80, one of the busiest stretches of blacktop in the southwestern United States. These days, old 80 is just a pothole plagued, dusty side-street, but because of the lyrics of a song, Rosa's Cantina became an unlikely but popular landmark. People from all over the world visit this little restaurant/bar. They come from Germany, Australia, even Russia to see the place made famous by a man named Marty Robbins.

In 1960, singer/songwriter Marty Robbins released a ballad he called "El Paso." It became one of the most popular recordings in country music history. In that song, Robbins mentions a tiny cafe, and Marty Robbins fanatics claim Rosa's was the cafe that inspired the song. As legend has it, Robbins eyeballed the place while on a road trip through West Texas, then wrote the song that some say put El Paso on the map. Marty Robbins died in the 80s, but his son Ronnie confirms the Rosa's rumors with this account:

"That was probably his all-time biggest hit. I remember a lot of the details from when he wrote it. We were on our way to Phoenix and my mother was driving and I was in the front seat with her. Daddy was in the back seat with his little Martin guitar that he used on stage and was just writing and singing these words that sounded like something that came out of a movie. It was just a neat story and he was incorporating things we were seeing on our trip. I don't really remember seeing Rosa's Cantina, but he was singing about

Stop #48

El Paso, Texas

"Robbins eyeballed the place while on a road trip through West Texas"

it as we were coming down off the hill overlooking El Paso. He sang that song all the way to Demming, New Mexico."

Rosa's put El Paso on the musical map.

So what some folks would call a hole in the wall was immortalized in a song. But Rosa's may not be there forever. What was a busy boulevard in the 50s today is a bypassed backstreet, and song or not, Rosa's Cantina is on a day-to-day lease on life. Once a year, Marty Robbins fans gather here to celebrate the country star's birthday, but once a year hardly pays the bills. In the meantime, you can visit Rosa's Cantina and experience the inspiration for a legendary song first-hand.

Rosa's is open for lunch Monday through Friday 11 - 1:45. The bar is open every day from 2 pm until the

last person leaves. 3454 Doniphan West. From I-10,
exit Mesa and go west, then south on Doniphan. 915-
833-0402

★ BOB'S BEST BETS ★

Funny how we keep finding out that things we
thought happened first "Back East" actually happened
first in Texas. Now we strike right to the heart of the
Pilgrims' pride as we tell you that Thanksgiving in
Plymouth, Massachusetts, was in fact a Johnny-come-
lately when it comes to festivals of thanks in the New
World. Seems one Don Juan de Oñate led the first
major colonization effort into what is now the United
States. He began this momentous journey in January
1598, nearly a quarter of a century before the
Mayflower sailed from England.

As the story goes, more than 400 brave and
courageous men, 130 of whom had their families with
them, made up the expedition. They had all their
worldly possessions packed on 83 ox-drawn, wooden
wheeled wagons and carts, and with between 7,000
and 8,000 horses, oxen, sheep, goats and cattle, formed
a four-mile-long procession through the desert! After
plodding across the desert for more than four months,
they arrived at the banks of the Rio Grande near
present day El Paso on April 20, 1598. After 10 days
of rest and recuperation, Don Juan ordered all of his
followers to put on their best clothing and gather for a
feast of thanksgiving. At that feast, Don Juan claimed
Texas on behalf of the King of Spain.

Almost 400 years later, El Pasoans celebrate the
"First Thanksgiving" with a festival and re-enactment
of the Spanish colonists' journey. The **First
Thanksgiving Pageant** takes place during the last
weekend of April and is free to the public. For more
information, contact the El Paso Mission Trail
Association at 800-351-6024.

Hueco Tanks, a place of mystery and majesty.

East of El Paso on U.S. 62/180 is a strange geological formation called **Hueco Tanks State Historical Park**. Hueco Tanks was a stopping place and camping ground for everyone from prehistoric peoples to 19th Century Native Americans. The niches, shelters and caves at the tanks provided places of religious ceremony and there is impressive artwork known as pictographs carved into the rocks. This was also the final stop on the Butterfield Stage before reaching El Paso. Great for a cultural visit or rock climbing. 915-857-1135

Across the Rio Grande from El Paso is its sister city, Juarez, Mexico's largest border city. **Juarez** is nestled in a valley in the Chihuahuan Desert and offers excellent shopping and an interesting cultural experience to visitors. There are lots of shops and restaurants, a mission dating to 1659 and a large traditional Mexican market. The easiest way to visit Juarez is to take the Border Jumper Trolley which leaves from the Civic Center in downtown El Paso.

If you are visiting El Paso the last half of December, be sure to take the **Christmas Trolley Tour of Lights**. The trolley takes you on the east side of the Franklin Mountains and provides a breathtaking view of both El Paso and Juarez. You will also pass through lots of neighborhoods lit with the candles in brown paper bags known as luminarias. 915-544-0062 or 800-259-6284

The Medicine Ball
Bounces Back

Stop #49

Fort Davis, Texas

Funny the twists and turns life offers that we never see coming our way. One day you're sitting in an office punching on a calculator or composing on a computer, the next day you've given it all up to ride fence on a cattle ranch. Actually, most of us only allow occasional dreams to momentarily sweep us away to a different life, then awake to the same old same old. Lineaus Lorette dreamed, then followed the dream all the way from Austin to Fort Davis.

Ever heard of a medicine ball? Chances are you've seen one, even if you didn't know what it was called. The medicine ball is an ancient Greek method of getting in shape, kind of an early day work-out machine. It's pretty simple really, just a leather ball that comes in various weights and sizes. The idea is to toss the ball around, preferably while walking, to exercise just about every muscle in your body. Well, Lineaus Lorette makes medicine balls. It's a far cry from his previous job as an Austin area accountant, but like we say, life is funny.

Lineaus' prescription for good health

Lineaus made his first medicine ball because he wanted one, and there aren't a lot of medicine ball makers around. Then he started making them for friends, and their friends, and soon he was in business. And since medicine ball making doesn't really require you to live in any particular place, he took advantage of the opportunities presented by his new life's calling and relocated to the place where he always wanted to live, Fort Davis, where the air is clear and the mall isn't crowded - because there isn't one! What could be better than that?

Drop by Lineaus Lorette's medicine ball factory for a tour of his facility and be sure to pick up a medicine ball while you're there. This is one of those things you just don't see much anymore. Call for an appointment. 800-626-6456

"Lineaus made his first medicine ball because he wanted one"

★ BOB'S BEST BETS ★

Fort Davis was one of the first military posts established in Texas for the purpose of guarding the 600 mile route through the wilderness between San Antonio and El Paso. In 1854, Fort Davis was established to offer some protection from the attacks and to patrol the route, protect the mail and wagon trains, and explore the territory.

Today, Fort Davis is an excellent example of frontier forts and includes both ruins and restorations. The fort is operated by the National Park Service and offers a museum in the reconstructed barracks, giving visitors a glimpse at the life of a frontier soldier. The fort is at the mouth of a box canyon on Limpia Creek and contains several adobe and stone buildings. The site covers 460 acres and offers several miles of hiking trails and a shaded picnic area. Summer hours are 8 - 6 daily. Winter hours are 8 - 5 daily. Small admission fee. On the north side of town on Texas Highway 118. 915-426-3224

When in Fort Davis, you'll probably want to commit

> "People in
> Fort Davis
> say this
> area is a
> little closer
> to heaven
> than other
> parts of
> Texas"

some minor crime just so you'll get booked in the local jail. Not your idea of a good time? Well, in Jeff Davis County they do things a little differently. The **Jeff Davis County Jail** served the county for 63 years. When time came to replace it, they didn't tear it down — they converted it into a library. The old cells are still there, but now they're filled with books. And that's like killing two birds with one stone - if you don't pay your fines when you return those overdue books, you're already in the slammer! On Main Street across from the courthouse. 915-426-3802

The **Neill Museum** on Court Avenue is also a bed and breakfast, but there are only two rooms available. The museum has more than 300 dolls from around the world as well as antique furniture. Admission fee. Open June through Labor Day Monday through Saturday 10 - 5, Sunday 1:30 - 5. 915-426-3969

People in Fort Davis say this area is a little closer to heaven than other parts of Texas. Technically speaking, they're right, because this is the highest incorporated town in Texas at just over 5,000 feet. But there is another reason for the saying — one named **McDonald Observatory**. When amateur astronomer William J. McDonald died, he left money in his will to build the observatory. The University of Texas McDonald Observatory at Mt. Locke was built in 1932 on a 6,791-foot peak about 16 miles from Fort Davis. The site was selected for all the reasons it was not put in some city location - clear air, cloudless nights, and very little artificial light. Next door, on adjacent Mount Fowlkes, an even newer telescope is now available.

The observatory is open 9 - 5 every day and offers daily guided tours at 2 pm and an additional morning tour during March and June through August. The self-guided tour and solar viewing area is free. Small fee for the guided tour. Evening public programs are held three times a week with a small admission fee. 915-426-3640

Don't travel all the way to Fort Davis and miss the **Scenic Loop**. This 74-mile drive will show you the incredible beauty of the area. Take Texas 17 just 2 miles south of Fort Davis to Texas Highway 166, then west to Texas Highway 118, then southeast back to Texas Highway 17 and back to Fort Davis. This incredible drive passes right by **Davis Mountains State Park**. Here you will find great camping and hiking and excellent views. If you plan to stay overnight, you will need to make advance reservations with the state park central booking office at 512-389-8900. Another fine option in the park is **Indian Lodge**, a pueblo-style motel built in the 1930s. 915-426-3254

On this same highway the scenic drive will take you past **Skillman Grove** where they've held the **Bloys Cowboy Camp Meetings** every year since 1890. This is an old-fashioned non-denominational outdoor revival. We met a man in Fort Davis recently who is in his 90s and has never missed a cowboy camp meeting!

If you want to spend some time in Fort Davis there are several outstanding overnight facilities. The **Hotel Limpia** is in the middle of the downtown area and is a restored 1912 hotel complete with antique furnishings. 915-426-3237

Just outside of town is the **Prude Ranch** where you can get a taste of the cowboy way of life, including pretty good cowboy cooking. By the way, if you are interested in birding, more than 150 different kinds of birds have been spotted in this area, and the folks at Prude Ranch offer special birding weeks for groups of 10 or more. 800-458-6232

If you are interested in the plant life of this area, the **Chihuahuan Desert Visitor Center** is located on Texas Highway 118 about 4 miles southwest of town. The center has botanic gardens and nature trails related to the desert flora. This is primarily a research center where they collect and study every plant that is native to the area. If it's growing somewhere in the desert, chances are it's growing here, too. Open April through August, Monday through Friday 1 - 5, Saturday and Sunday 9 - 6. 915-837-8370

"If it's growing somewhere in the desert, chances are it's growing here, too"

Art In The Desert

I've mentioned before how we love to find things in small towns that you might expect to find only in big cities. It is no surprise to find Confederate monuments on courthouse squares in small Texas towns. It is no surprise to stumble on old drugstores with soda fountains in small Texas towns. It is a surprise to find a world class modern art museum in a small Texas town. Welcome to Marfa, home of the Chinati Foundation.

Brush back the dust of this tiny desert community and you will see an art mecca. It is a place dedicated to light, color and space. It is a place offered as an alternative to the traditional museum. Surrounded by the desert landscape of Presidio County just 60 miles north of the Mexican border, the specific purpose of this place is to provide a location for the permanent installation of large contemporary works of art.

The Chinati Foundation was created and founded by the late Donald Judd. Besides his own work, the museum includes the art of Carl Andre, Ingolfur Arnarsson, John Chamberlain, Roni Horn, Ilya Kabakov, Richard Long, Claes Oldenburg, David Rabinowitch and Hyong-Keun Yun. The foundation also operates supporting programs and facilities

Stop #50

Marfa, Texas

"Donald Judd took an instrument of war and transformed it into an instrument of art"

From army outpost to high-brow art museum

148

including a printmaking studio, artists' residences, special temporary exhibitions, college and university internships, children's art classes, seminars and concerts. All of this is in what some would say is the least likely of locations.

Long before the walls of the Chinati Foundation housed a spectacular art collection, they imprisoned German soldiers. This museum was once Fort D. A. Russell, an army post on the edge of town. Donald Judd took an instrument of war and transformed it into an instrument of art. Some say that without these particular buildings the work within them might not be as powerful; that the space and light are themselves works of art. That, combined with the big, open sky and miles of desert terrain seem to form the ideal setting for art. Donald Judd said, "Somewhere a portion of contemporary art has to exist as an example of what the art and its context were meant to be. Somewhere, just as the platinum-iridium meter guarantees the tape measure, a strict measure must exist for the art of this time and place."

The Chinati Foundation/La Fundacion Chinati is located at 1 Cavalry Row just off Highway 67 in Marfa. Open Thursday through Saturday 1 - 5 and by appointment. Free admission. 915-729-4362

★ BOB'S BEST BETS ★

Marfa is best known for two things: the **Marfa Mystery Lights** and as the location for the filming of the 1955 movie **"Giant"** starring Rock Hudson, James Dean and Elizabeth Taylor.

The Marfa Lights are real. We know because we have seen them time and again. As for exactly what they are, we don't know. No one knows. But drive east out of town about 9 miles on U.S. Highway 90/67 and you will see the official viewing area. Every night, folks who have traveled here from all over the world gather to see what they can see. Look southwest toward the Chinati Mountains and suddenly they will appear. First you will see a bright ball of light moving slightly, then it may split into two balls. Then another. The show goes on all night long just like that. Native Americans reported seeing the lights 150 years ago, so we know they are not electrical. Pilots reported seeing the lights during World War II when there was an airbase here, so the sightings are not random or unreliable. Scientists have studied them for years and confirm something is out there but admit they don't know what. And we have videotaped them, offering proof positive of their existence. If you're in the area around Labor Day, you'll enjoy the **Marfa Lights Festival** which includes all the typical small town festival fun. For more information contact the Marfa Chamber of Commerce at 915-729-4942.

The **El Paisano Hotel** in downtown Marfa is where most of the cast and crew of Giant lived during the movie's filming. The big stars stayed in private homes in town and Marfa was a beehive of activity for weeks. The hotel is a beautiful 1927 structure in which three presidents have stayed (Roosevelt, Truman and Kennedy) along with lots of movie stars and other celebrities. Inside the lobby you will find Giant memorabilia inside glass cabinets. 915-729-3145

In nearby Alpine, just 26 miles east of Marfa (keep in mind that anything under 100 miles is "nearby" in this part of Texas) you'll find **Sul Ross University** and the **Museum of the Big Bend**. There is a collection of artifacts here dating back to the Native Americans who first inhabited this region, continuing through the Spanish explorers, cavalry and cowboys. Open Tuesday through Saturday 9 - 5, Sundays 1 - 5. On the campus of Sul Ross (Entrance #2 from Highway 90). Free admission. 915-837-8143

Also in Alpine is our favorite radio station in the entire state. **KVLF** (Voice of the Last Frontier) is operated by Ray Hendryx and his daddy founded the station. We would tell you the frequency so you could listen while in the area but it's unnecessary. Just hit "scan" on the car radio and KVLF is the only AM station you'll find anywhere in the Big Bend area! Okay, so you have an older model without the "scan" feature. Tune in AM 1240. And be sure that old car is in good repair because service stations out here are few and far between.

There is a refreshing simplicity to small town radio, but this particular station is the cream of the crop. Ray Hendryx is the station manager, morning DJ, engineer, maintenance man and sometimes floor sweeper. He keeps goats outside the small building where the KVLF studios are located just to keep the grass around the transmitter mowed. The format? Whatever Ray likes, but definitely no trashy talk and no rap. Just lots of country and tunes from the 30s, 40s and 50s mostly, with some local news, weather (it's always the same) and sports thrown in. It's also a good deal because you can buy a one minute commercial for as little as $4.45. Take our word for it and don't miss listening to KVLF while you're here.

The hills and valleys in this area have been home to cattle ranching for so long no one can remember which came first — the cowboy or the cactus. But half a century ago cattle prices were as jumpy as a jackrabbit in a prairie fire. Back then, Frank Woodward realized it would take more than beef to keep the family ranch. It would take a miracle, like all the worthless rocks in his pastures turning into gold. That's when Frank hit pay dirt, and soon folks were calling Frank's place The Rock Ranch.

The **Woodward Rock Ranch**, south of Alpine 16 miles on Texas Highway 118, offers 4,000 acres of agates, stones exploding with plumes of fiery complexion. They were born in volcanic lava 43 million years ago and lay like hidden treasure in otherwise ordinary looking stone. Cut and polished, they erupt into a kaleidoscope of color. That's why folks pay to cart some of them off when they find them here. They charge 50 cents a pound if you find something you want to keep. Looking is free. Open 8 AM 'til dark every day. 915-364-2271

"There is a refreshing simplicity to small town radio"

The Legacy of a Big Bend Legend

Stop #51
Marathon, Texas

"A collection of memories gathered from the dusty attic and sharp mind of a West Texas cowgirl"

Big Bend. Vast, legendary and unchanged by the river of time. It is a rugged, yet peaceful corner of the earth. And it is the place Hallie Stillwell has called home for almost 90 years.

In the grand scheme of things in a place as old as time itself, 90 years is but a flash of an instant. But Hallie Stillwell has been here for almost that long, and she's seen and done more things than most of us could do in two lifetimes. She's outlived, outdone and overcome every obstacle in her path and become a legend in the meantime. It's hard to imagine a little old lady taming the frontier, but don't be fooled. Hallie is a tough as nails pioneer who was riding and roping before most of us were born. And during all her adventures, Hallie realized this place is unlike anywhere else on earth - a beautiful place that should be seen and experienced by everyone.

In a little building off Farm Road 2627 Hallie Stillwell's story is told. Hallie's Hall of Fame is a collection of memories gathered from the dusty attic and sharp mind of a West Texas cowgirl. From lanterns to lightbulbs and saddles to sedans, Hallie has watched the world around her change. Separately, all this stuff in her Hall of Fame might not be much, but together it tells an important story about one unique woman and her unmatched view of the world.

The story goes that there's not a trail for a hundred miles that Hallie hasn't ridden on horseback. When we first met her a few years back she was still packin' a pistol, just in case a rattler wouldn't say no. Today, Hallie is taking things a little slower, but you can still relive her life at Hallie's Hall of Fame. Six miles from the eastern entrance to Big Bend National Park on FM 2627 and 46 miles south of Marathon, which is the nearest town via route 385. Stop in at the Stillwell Store next door and get the key, then take the self-guided tour. Admission is free, but donations are appreciated. Hallie's daughter, Dadie, will be happy to give group tours and programs by appointment. 915-376-2244

Marathon's ode to a cowgirl

★ BOB'S BEST BETS ★

In 1878, an 18-year-old Vermont native left the comfort of his East Coast home to make his fortune on the western frontier. He landed in Texas and became a prosperous banker and rancher in San Antonio. Alfred Gage frequented the area around Marathon, Texas, as he traveled there to check on his 500,000 acre ranch, so he decided to build a hotel that would also serve as

his ranch headquarters. Today, that hotel is the
landmark of this town as much as the Space Needle is
the landmark of Seattle and the Eiffel Tower is the
landmark of Paris.

The **Gage Hotel** was restored to its original
greatness in 1982, and every effort was made during
the renovation to recreate the atmosphere of the cattle-
dominated Trans-Pecos at the turn of the century. The
sunsets are unmatched and the food in the dining room
is memorable. 800-884-GAGE

The wide open spaces of Big Bend

After you've visited Hallie Stillwell's place south of
Marathon, you'll want to continue on into **Big Bend
National Park**. Go first to Panther Junction which
serves as the visitors' center and park headquarters.
There you will find all kinds of information about the
park: where to go, what to do, what to watch out for. If
you plan to do any hiking or camping while you're
here, check the weather forecast just to be sure. Flash
floods are deadly in the area.

Go east from Panther Junction to a little spot near Rio Grande Village where you can cross the river to the Mexican town of **Boquillas**. For about two bucks a Mexican citizen will take you across the river in a row boat where you will have your choice of a donkey or the bed of a pick-up for the trip up to town on the top of the hill. That will cost you another two or three bucks. You can get simple Mexican food at the little restaurant, explore the town in just a few minutes and visit the bar that's right out of a spaghetti western. This is technically an illegal crossing from the United States into Mexico, but border patrols on both sides have long looked the other way and allowed this cultural exchange to take place.

After crossing back into the U.S., ask around to get directions to the **Hot Springs**, a place a mile or two off the main road where there is hot water bubbling out of the ground in a tub on the banks of the river. Usually there are tourists sitting there and it's a great place to strike up a conversation about nothing while you bask in the hot sun and hot water.

Travel back to the west to the center of the park and **Chisos Basin**. This is actually a 1,500 foot depression in the Chisos Mountains where you'll find the **Chisos Mountains Lodge**. Don't expect to get a room here unless you've booked it in advance, but the restaurant offers pretty good food. The hiking trails here offer breathtaking views. The wildlife is abundant and places like The Window and Mule Ear Peaks provide photo opportunities you won't find elsewhere.

In the southeast part of the park you'll find the village of **Castolon**. Deserted cavalry barracks and a little store is about all there is here, but you can picnic at nearby **Cottonwood Campground**.

Big Bend National Park is more than 800,000 acres and it would take years to see it all, and these are just a few simple suggestions for where you might start. The best months to visit are October, November, and April, but it's an interesting place at any time of the year. Contact the visitors' center at 915-477-2251.

A Far Flung Adventure

Stop #52

Terlingua, Texas

"This truly is the last frontier"

Since we started our journey of the Lone Star State where Texas began, it is only appropriate to finish it where Texas ends. You could argue, of course, that such a spot could be at any place on her border. We believe the "end of Texas" happens on the Rio Grande, out in the rough and rugged wide open spaces of a place called Mariscal Canyon. This is the bend in Big Bend, the southernmost dip of the river where it cuts through limestone walls that jut up like giant buildings, rising out of the ground like some ancient skyscraper.

Places like Mariscal are most easily experienced from the water, and the only way we advise anyone to do that is by way of a river raft adventure through a reputable outfitter. There are several, but our favorite is Far Flung Adventures in Terlingua. The others may be every bit as qualified and dependable, but we know the folks at Far Flung, having been down the river with them on many occasions, and we know we can count on them to deliver our friends and readers safe and sound.

You can customize your rafting trip to suit your desires, but the most popular last anywhere from a half-day (probably through Santa Elena Canyon) to one or two nights. In this amount of time you can experience just about everything the river and the canyons have to offer short of long-range hiking and serious climbing, which we recommend only to the most experienced in these areas. You'll meet the Far Flung folks in the morning at Terlingua Ghost Town (more on this later) and begin your journey with a long and wild van trip to the river. By the time you arrive you will already feel like you have surely pioneered something, though you have yet to get in a raft on the water. Your river guides will feed you lunch on the banks of the Rio Grande while they ready the boats and supplies. Then you'll be off on an adventure like no other.

Don't expect white water on the Rio Grande. In fact, don't even expect deep water. Most of the time there will be places where your guide and rower will step into the water and push the raft over an area of shallow water, but rarely will you have to help. Soon you will

Who needs white water with this view!

reach the towering walls of the canyon and only then will you understand why this must be the end of Texas. You will be farther from a commercial airport than from any other spot in the lower 48. There are no cell phone towers, no way to reach 9-1-1, not even a road to carry you out. This truly is the last frontier. Were you alone here, you would never be as alone anywhere else.

The guys and gals at Far Flung (it's owned by Mike Davidson and his wife, Gay, who often rows a boat) offer up lots of interesting information during your journey and some pretty good grub during your stops.

Overnight camping will be professionally handled and as easy as possible, and there is often even some good entertainment along with you. On one of our trips, professional balladeer and star of the Texas Music craze of the 70s Steve Fromholz was actually our rower and guide.

If you are really looking for something different, book one of the special trips featuring San Antonio chef Francois Maeder. He brings along an incredible array of gourmet food and sometimes, Texas heat permitting, even serves in white tux and tails, right there in the most remote area you have ever visited. This special gourmet trip is expensive, but if you're looking for something different, this might be the trip for you. 800-359-4138

★ BOB'S BEST BETS ★

Back to Terlingua. This was once a mining town after mercury was discovered in 1890 and hundreds of shacks housed a population of more than 2,000 people. Millions of dollars worth of quicksilver were marketed before the boom tapered off. All of the old wooden shacks from that day are gone now, but there are still plenty of roofless adobe buildings to be seen. The old cemetery in **Terlingua Ghost Town** has some markers which tell interesting stories, but there are probably more people buried there than actually live in Terlingua today. Once a year though the population of this town swells to more than 5,000 when "chili heads" from around the world convene for the annual **Frank X. Tolbert/Wick Fowler Memorial Championship Chili Cookoff**, started in 1967. We first visited this event at the invitation of our old friend and mentor Frank X. Tolbert, and found it to be one of the most bizarre festivals of any kind in the state. Always held the first weekend in November.

If you're looking for food in Terlingua, try the **Starlight Theatre Restaurant**. It's an old movie house that looks like it's built into the side of a mountain. Sometimes the "desert people" come into town and perform their poetry, songs and other entertainment for one another and for the tourists who happen to be visiting. The food here is so-so. The service is even worse (they say former Governor Ann Richards had to get up and get her own ice tea refills) but the atmosphere makes the place worth putting up with for an evening. Another spot you'll want to try is **La Kiva**, a strange place that you just have to see with a beautiful patio and a dining room built into the side of Terlingua Creek in a kind of cave.

In the morning, try the **Roadrunner Deli** in Study Butte, just down the road from Terlingua. The food at this place is very good, and the muffins and pancakes are some of the best we've eaten anywhere. Open when they're open, closed when they decide to.

Thirteen miles down the road from Terlingua is **Lajitas on the Rio Grande**. This is not an old Texas town, though it would appear so at first glance. It's actually a resort made to look like an old Texas border town. Visit the **Lajitas Trading Post**, which has operated since 1899, to stock up on supplies and conversation. Roger Gibson is actually a city boy who took over the place a few years ago and he has lots of different things for sale both inside and out back and lots of great stories. You may want to pick up a "tinaja" (ti-NA-ha) while you're there. These are volcanic rock vessels fashioned by Mexicans from huge mountainside stones and brought to the trading post by Roger. Whatever you do, don't feed beer to the goat at the trading post. This is a popular college prank kind of stunt that some folks think is cute, but we assure you it's bad for the goat. Open daily 7 - 8. 915-424-3234

"It's here that we'll leave you"

It's here that we'll leave you. Thanks for traveling the state with us, whether you've been a companion for the more than quarter-century we've been sending back stories via our weekly television program or you've just joined us for this book. Either way, we've enjoyed your company and hope you feel the same love as we do for the greatest state in the country - Texas!

NOTES